Talent Management for U.S. Department of Defense Knowledge Workers

What Does RAND Corporation Research Tell Us?

LAURA WERBER

Prepared for the Office of the Secretary of Defense
Approved for public release; distribution unlimited

NATIONAL DEFENSE RESEARCH INSTITUTE

For more information on this publication, visit www.rand.org/t/RRA950-1

Library of Congress Cataloging-in-Publication Data is available for this publication.
ISBN: 978-1-9774-0682-8

Published by the RAND Corporation, Santa Monica, Calif.
© Copyright 2021 RAND Corporation
RAND® is a registered trademark.

Cover images: metamorworks/Getty Images; Vonkara1/Getty Images.

Support RAND
Make a tax-deductible charitable contribution at
www.rand.org/giving/contribute

www.rand.org

Preface

This report features a synthesis of findings from publicly available RAND Corporation reports funded by the U.S. Department of Defense (DoD) pertaining to knowledge worker talent management published since 2013—when its report on improving the diversity of the U.S. Department of Defense (DoD) science, technology, engineering, and mathematics (STEM) workforce and a related report on the implementation of DoD's diversity and inclusion strategic plan were released—through mid-2020. Findings are mapped on to four pillars of talent management: build and organize, train and develop, manage and motivate performance, and promote and retain the right talent. The report also identifies potentially overlooked topics and opportunities for future research. It should primarily be of interest to DoD personnel involved with civilian manpower/personnel policy issues but also of value to personnel from other government agencies whose responsibilities include talent management.

The research reported here was completed in January 2021 and underwent security review with the sponsor and the Defense Office of Prepublication and Security Review before public release.

This research was sponsored by the Office of the Secretary of Defense and conducted within the Forces and Resources Policy Center of the RAND National Security Research Division, which operates the RAND National Defense Research Institute, a federally funded research and development center sponsored by the Office of the Secretary of Defense, the Joint Staff, the Unified Combatant Commands, the Navy, the Marine Corps, the defense agencies, and the defense intelligence enterprise.

For more information on the Forces and Resources Policy Center, see www.rand.org/nsrd/frp or contact the director. (Contact information is provided on the webpage.)

Contents

Preface iii

Summary vii

Abbreviations xv

CHAPTER ONE
Introduction 1

CHAPTER TWO
Approach 3

CHAPTER THREE
Build and Organize 7
Workforce Requirements. 7
Recruiting and Hiring. 12
Workforce Composition. 17

CHAPTER FOUR
Train and Develop 21
Training and Development for Specific Types of
    Knowledge Workers. 21
Learning from the Private Sector. 24
Assessment and Evaluation. 26

CHAPTER FIVE
Motivate and Manage Performance...29
Financial Incentives..29
Nonfinancial Incentives..31
Additional Strategies to Sustain or Improve Performance 32

CHAPTER SIX
Promote and Retain the Right Talent.....................................35
Characteristics of Those Promoted 35
Characteristics of Those Retained 37
Policy and Strategy Influences on Retention 39

CHAPTER SEVEN
Data Issues Present Challenges to Effective Talent Management..... 43

Conclusion 47

APPENDIXES
**A. Annotated Bibliography of Selected RAND Defense Talent
Management Studies, 2013–2020** 51

References 77

Summary

Effective talent management of the defense workforce, particularly civilians and those performing knowledge work, has become an imperative in recent years, as evidenced by references to various aspects of talent management in the *2018 National Defense Strategy*, the *President's Management Agenda*, and the FY 2020 National Defense Authorization Act. The RAND Corporation has conducted many studies focused on this topic, and this report summarizes findings from 31 publicly available RAND reports published since 2013—when its report on improving the diversity of the U.S. Department of Defense (DoD) science, technology, engineering, and mathematics (STEM) workforce and a related report on the implementation of DoD's diversity and inclusion strategic plan were released—through mid-2020.

In the process of reviewing the publications and mapping their key findings and recommendations to talent management topics, the author developed a framework to organize themes and provide a comprehensive view of talent management, one correspondent with the U.S. Officer of Personnel Management's (OPM) human capital framework. The RAND framework includes four pillars of talent management:

- **build and organize:** research about the numbers and types of knowledge workers required; the required competencies or knowledge, skills, abilities, and other characteristics (KSAO); recruiting and hiring; and workforce composition
- **train and develop:** research about the necessary training and development (T&D) for defense knowledge workers, sources of that T&D, and evaluation of T&D

- **motivate and manage performance:** research about financial and nonfinancial performance incentives as well as other strategies to sustain or improve performance
- **promote and retain the right talent:** research about the characteristics of those more or less likely to be promoted, the characteristics of those more or less likely to remain with DoD, and factors that may influence retention.

Diversity management was a theme that cut across these four areas, with studies featuring observations related to recruitment, development, and/or retention of such groups as women, racial and ethnic minorities, and people with targeted disabilities (PWTD). Various concerns related to data systems or data were identified frameworkwide as well.

Build and Organize

RAND research reflected DoD struggles with defining required capabilities and job classifications for personnel with responsibilities related to cyber, data science, and security cooperation. Studies also revealed issues pertaining to defining business-related knowledge (e.g., knowledge of industry operations, knowledge of industry motivation) and STEM, codifying the needs for business-related knowledge within the defense acquisition workforce, and determining manning requirements for STEM-degree personnel. Researchers not only identified these areas of concern but also presented such solutions as a working definition for STEM, position descriptions for data science specialties, and draft competency models for software and security cooperation. They also underscored the importance of understanding how malleable required competencies are, so that those less amenable to improvement via T&D were considered part of the candidate selection process.

Additional findings intended to help DoD build its workforce pertained to recruiting and hiring. For example, researchers described how pay-related concerns may affect DoD efforts to recruit STEM candidates and cyberpersonnel and, in one study, examined DoD's use of pay-setting flexibilities to hire acquisition personnel. They also looked to the private sector for promising strategies to help with DoD civilian recruiting and selection in general and for cyberpersonnel in particular. Employee referral bonuses, company branding, and savvy use of social media all could help to attract talent, whereas such screening tools as hackathons could help to gauge both technical talent and passion.

Train and Develop

Opportunities to improve T&D for several technical types of knowledge workers—those in data science, software, and cyber—were described in several studies, and educational opportunities for acquisition workforce personnel and supervisors were covered as well. Educational activities outside DoD, including not only coursework from colleges and universities but also professional certifications and industry-based rotations, tended to be regarded favorably by subject matter experts. However, some had limited value due to capacity constraints. In addition, it was challenging to gauge their usefulness due to both the lack of clarity about desired capabilities or knowledge noted earlier and limited efforts by DoD to evaluate the effectiveness of various T&D initiatives. Several studies offered ways to improve DoD's capacity for evaluating T&D activities, including identifying measures for specific competencies that may be important for different types of knowledge work, such as adaptability, critical thinking, and creative problem solving.

Manage and Motivate Performance

Studies that fell in this category covered financial incentives, nonfinancial incentives, and other strategies for maximizing employee performance. Lessons from the private sector suggest that financial incentives could be motivating, particularly spot bonuses and other merit-based awards, but RAND's analysis of the Civilian Acquisition Workforce

Personnel Demonstration Project (AcqDemo) personnel demonstration project suggests that DoD may not be making the best use of such awards. Nonfinancial incentives, such as meaningful work and the opportunity for lifelong learning, were regarded as powerful incentives for knowledge workers as well, perhaps more influential than financial incentives in some instances. Other tools and strategies available to DoD to promote strong performance for knowledge workers include the use of ongoing check-ins, employee resource groups or affinity groups, and decentralized organizational structure.

Promote and Retain the Right Talent

Findings that fall under this talent management pillar include those about promotion outcomes, retention outcomes, and strategies to improve the latter. Although General Schedule (GS) performance ratings data have their limitations, such as a lack of variance across the defense workforce, one study team was able to use them in analysis that indicated higher average performance ratings were associated with a lower likelihood of retention. When RAND researchers focused on AcqDemo, which had more detailed performance ratings data, they found that employees with high contribution scores were more likely to be promoted and were more likely to be retained than were employees with low contribution scores.

Some of the studies in this research stream indicate that compensation in the form of high pay or retention bonuses may not be as useful for retention, at least based on insights from the private sector. Instead, the same nonfinancial factors cited as ways to inspire strong performance, such as meaningful work, regular opportunities for career development, and affinity groups, were also regarded as helping with retention, along with mentoring and opportunities for promotion. A simulation model revealed, however, that a pay *freeze*, especially one of uncertain length, could have a potentially large effect on retention for both the overall GS workforce and the GS STEM workforce in particular. Finally, one study considered retention from a different angle, reminding DoD not only to retain the right talent but also to address the problem of poor-performing employees, particularly by improving supervisors' use of tools, policies, and procedures intended for that purpose.

Managing Diversity

RAND research suggested some challenges related to the diversity of the defense acquisition workforce. A 2013 study indicated that the share of women in the DoD civilian STEM workforce was far lower than the share in the overall U.S. STEM workforce (using a definition that included health practitioners), and this gender gap was not explained by differences in educational attainment. A later study found that women were underrepresented in the DoD civilian workforce compared with the non-DoD federal workforce and the U.S. labor force. This gender gap was due in part to veteran status, with women less likely to be veterans. Turning our attention to career outcomes, women in AcqDemo experience fewer promotions than did their counterparts in the GS system, but in separate analysis of promotions to the Senior Executive Service (SES), gender was not a predictor of promotion. Finally, within AcqDemo, women were retained at lower rates than men, but that was also true of the equivalent GS population and of the DoD civilian workforce overall.

Looking at racial and ethnic diversity, the DoD civilian STEM workforce had a slightly higher Black population and similar Hispanic population to the overall U.S. STEM workforce. In another study in which researchers looked at the overall DoD civilian workforce, they found that Hispanics were underrepresented in the DoD civilian workforce compared with the non-DoD federal workforce and the U.S. labor force. These differences were partially explained by differences in observable characteristics, but the study team also identified various barriers to greater levels of Hispanic employment, including the geographic location of many positions, perceived language or citizenship concerns, the complexity of the USAJOBS application process, and lack of awareness and motivation by DoD leadership to address this issue.

Career outcomes for racial and ethnic minorities within the defense workforce varied by demographic group and across studies as well. RAND researchers determined that nonwhite employees under AcqDemo, the majority of whom was Black, experienced fewer promotions than did their GS system counterparts. Within AcqDemo, researchers found no differences in promotion rates between white employees and Black employees, white employees and Asian employees, or non-Hispanic and Hispanic employees after taking other measurable factors into account. Race was not a significant predictor of promotion to SES, due at least in part to underrepresentation in the career fields that have a disproportionate number of SES. Across DoD overall, Hispanics tended to work in occupations with lower rates of promotion, and those who do work in high-promoting occupations are less likely to be promoted than non-Hispanic employees. The authors of that study also found that Hispanics constituted a greater share of separations than of new hires. In a related vein, another study team reported that Hispanic personnel covered by AcqDemo were retained at lower rates than their non-Hispanic counterparts. In contrast, Black and Asian personnel in AcqDemo were retained at higher rates than their white counterparts.

Concluding Observations

Overall, RAND research has much to tell policymakers and analysts about knowledge worker talent management. Some efforts addressed a specific type of knowledge workers, most often those with cyberskills. In many cases, researchers identified areas in need of improvement, but they also proposed solutions and identified ways for DoD to take a proactive approach to talent management. The private sector and DoD experiments, such as the Defense Acquisition Workforce Development Fund (DAWDF) and AcqDemo, were commonly cited sources of promising practices.

This review also uncovered gaps in RAND's DoD-sponsored research. Many of the studies focused on building the defense workforce and retaining the right talent; there was considerably less research attention paid to managing and motivating personnel. Moreover, there were very few findings about supervisors and none at the team or work group level. Finally, evaluation-oriented studies were limited, with AcqDemo assessments and an evaluation of the Army's Asymmetric Warfare Adaptive Leader Program the notable exceptions. Given that multiple studies suggested ways in which DoD's approach to evaluation fell short, future research centered on evaluation would be an especially constructive way to strengthen talent management of knowledge workers in the DoD civilian workforce.

Abbreviations

360s	360-degree review
AcqDemo	Civilian Acquisition Workforce Personnel Demonstration Project
ALRM	Army Leader Requirements Model
DAWDF	Defense Acquisition Workforce Development Fund
DIA	Defense Intelligence Agency
DoD	U.S. Department of Defense
GS	General Schedule
IT	information technology
KSA	knowledge, skills, and abilities
KSAO	knowledge, skills, abilities, and other characteristics
OPM	U.S. Office of Personnel Management
PWTD	people with targeted disabilities
SES	Senior Executive Service
STEM	science, technology, engineering, and mathematics
T&D	training and development

CHAPTER ONE

Introduction

General Creighton Abrams once said, "People are not in the Army. They are the Army."[1] That aphorism extends to the U.S. Department of Defense (DoD) more generally; its personnel are among its most important assets. Perhaps in recognition of that truth, policymakers and DoD leaders are increasingly focused on the defense workforce. The *2018 National Defense Strategy* states that "[r]ecruiting, developing, and retaining a high-quality military and civilian workforce is essential for warfighting success" and notes the importance of talent management and cultivating civilian workforce expertise in particular.[2] Around the same time frame, the *President's Management Agenda* stated that DoD, along with the U.S. Office of Personnel Management (OPM) and U.S. Office of Management and Budget,[3] would lead the federal government to achieve a cross-agency priority goal: developing the federal workforce for the 21st century. This goal was to be accomplished via active management of the workforce in terms of performance management and employee engagement, increased agility in reallocating human capital resources, and streamlined ways to attract and hire top talent. Another *President's Management Agenda* cross-agency goal called for DoD and other federal agencies to develop staff

---

[1] Pete Gere, "Secretary of the Army Statement on the Army's Strategic Imperatives," Testimony Before the Senate Armed Services Committee, United States Senate, First Session, 110th Congress, Washington, D.C., November 15, 2007.

[2] U.S. Department of Defense, *Summary of the 2018 National Defense Strategy: Sharpening the American Military's Competitive Edge*, Washington, D.C., 2018, pp. 7–8.

[3] The White House, *President's Management Agenda*, Washington, D.C., 2018.

capabilities to better leverage data as a strategic asset. Most recently, in the FY 2020 National Defense Authorization Act, Congress turned its attention to DoD workforce issues in several sections, mandating the establishment of a Defense Civilian Training Corps, the creation of a new approach to certifications for the defense acquisition workforce, reports on the department's use of probationary periods for the civilian workforce, and greater efforts to diversify the department's research and engineering workforce.

Concurrent with this heightened attention to the federal workforce, particularly civilians and those performing knowledge work in science, technology, engineering, and mathematics (STEM) or acquisition career fields,[4] the RAND Corporation has conducted many studies focusing on defense workforce management issues. This body of work spans research sponsors, including those in the U.S. Army, U.S. Air Force, and Office of the Secretary of Defense, and addresses topics related to attracting, developing, managing, and retaining talent. In this report, I summarize findings from 31 publicly available RAND reports published from 2013 through mid-2020 to highlight key themes with implications for management of knowledge workers within DoD and other national security organizations.

---

[4] Following Drucker, I define knowledge work as work that entails applying specialized theoretical and analytic knowledge, typically acquired via formal education, to produce goods and services. See Peter F. Drucker, "The Age of Social Transformation," *The Atlantic Monthly*, Vol. 274, No. 5, 1994.

CHAPTER TWO

Approach

The review focused on publicly released RAND publications about the defense workforce from 2013, the year that its reports on improving DoD STEM workforce diversity and the implementation of DoD's diversity and inclusion strategic plan were published,[1] through the first half of 2020. Search terms were developed based on

1. OPM's definition of talent management, as included in the agency's human capital framework: "A system that promotes a high-performing workforce, identifies and closes skills gaps, and implements and maintains programs to attract, acquire, develop, promote, and retain quality and diverse talent."[2]
2. RAND's internal taxonomy of research topics.

They included but were not limited to talent management topics such as recruiting, hiring, training, education, career development, leader development, performance management, compensation, promotion, retention, diversity, and STEM. In addition to keyword searches, the

---

[1] Nelson Lim, Abigail Haddad, Dwayne M. Butler, and Katheryn Giglio, *First Steps Toward Improving DoD STEM Workforce Diversity: Response to the 2012 Department of Defense STEM Diversity Summit*, Santa Monica, Calif.: RAND Corporation, RR-329-OSD, 2013; and Nelson Lim, Abigail Haddad, and Lindsay Daugherty, *Implementation of the DoD Diversity and Inclusion Strategic Plan: A Framework for Change Through Accountability*, Santa Monica, Calif.: RAND Corporation, RR 333-OSD, 2013.

[2] U.S. Office of Personnel Management, "Human Capital Framework: Overview, Talent Management," webpage, undated.

author also examined curated pages on the RAND website in which RAND reports were organized by topic (e.g., civilian military workforce, military education and training). This search yielded 31 publications judged as pertaining to DoD knowledge workers, civilian or military, or with implications for knowledge work commissioned by a wide array of DoD sponsors, including those in the U.S. Air Force, U.S. Army, the Office of the Secretary of Defense, and the defense intelligence community. The publications and their abstracts are provided in the report's appendix. To ensure that no pertinent studies were missing, this annotated bibliography was shared with RAND subject-matter experts for feedback.

After the set of publications for inclusion was finalized, the author reviewed all the publications and used qualitative data analysis software to group related findings and recommendations by workforce management topic. Through an iterative process of reviewing publications and mapping them to workforce management topics, the author developed a framework for organizing and presenting related findings. This framework covers four pillars of talent management:

- **build and organize:** research about the numbers and types of knowledge workers required; the required competencies or knowledge, skills, abilities, and other characteristics (KSAOs); recruiting and hiring; and workforce composition
- **train and develop:** research about the necessary training and development (T&D) for defense knowledge workers, sources of that T&D, and evaluation of T&D
- **motivate and manage performance:** research about financial and nonfinancial performance incentives as well as other strategies to sustain or improve performance
- **promote and retain the right talent:** research about the characteristics of those more or less likely to be promoted, the characteristics of those more or less likely to remain with DoD, and factors that may influence retention.

These areas correspond to a degree with OPM's six focus areas for talent management: workforce planning, recruitment and outreach, employee development, leader development, retention, and knowledge management.[3] Workforce planning and recruitment and outreach are both captured under the build and organize pillar; employee development and leader development are part of train and develop; retention is included in promote and retain the right talent. OPM includes strategies to cultivate a motivated and engaged workforce under its retention focus area, but I opted to feature such research in a separate section, motivate and manage performance. Finally, the OPM talent management focus area knowledge management pertains to having a systematic approach to evaluation. Findings related to program or system evaluation were relatively limited, pertaining primarily to T&D, so they are included in that pillar.

In the next sections, key observations from the reviewed RAND publications are presented using the four pillars for organization. Following that, the report covers diversity management and data-related issues that cut across this framework. The report closes with a discussion of potentially overlooked topics and opportunities for future research.

---

[3] U.S. Office of Personnel Management, undated.

CHAPTER THREE

Build and Organize

Most of the studies included in this review in some way addressed building and organizing DoD's workforce. Taken together, they identified problems, solutions, and opportunities related to the number and types of people required to support DoD's mission, the necessary KSAOs and competencies, and recruiting and hiring practices. A few studies focused on the composition of DoD's workforce, covering such topics as its growth and other changes over time and the representation of women, racial and ethnic minorities, and people with targeted disabilities (PWTD) therein.

Workforce Requirements

Turning our attention first to the number and types of different knowledge workers required, several studies described vagueness in how career fields and job categories were defined for four increasingly important areas: cyber,[1]

---

[1] Martin C. Libicki, David Senty, and Julia Pollak, *Hackers Wanted: An Examination of the Cybersecurity Labor Market*, Santa Monica, Calif: RAND Corporation, RR-430, 2014; Christopher Paul, Isaac R. Porche III, and Elliot Axelband, *The Other Quiet Professionals: Lessons for Future Cyber Forces from the Evolution of Special Forces*, Santa Monica, Calif.: RAND Corporation, RR-780-A, 2014; Isaac R. Porche III, Caolionn O'Connell, John S. Davis II, Bradley Wilson, Chad C. Serena, Tracy C. McCausland, Erin-Elizabeth Johnson, Brian D. Wisniewski, and Michael Vasseur, *Cyber Power Potential of the Army's Reserve Component*, Santa Monica, Calif.: RAND Corporation, RR-1490-A, 2017.

requirements for STEM degrees and other types of college degrees.[15] As part of their work for the Defense Intelligence Agency (DIA),[16] Knopp and his team developed position descriptions for four emerging data science specialties, which in turn facilitated determining what the agency needed to build a robust data science capability. In another study, the team drafted a software competency model and offered guidance on how to validate it once DoD identifies its software workforce.[17] Markel and his colleagues carried out a similar effort for the defense security cooperation workforce, observing that it appeared to be divided into four different job families: international affairs, security assistance implementation management, international training management, and financial management.[18] They also identified security cooperation-specific competencies, including five that seemed common to almost every job. Several studies identified possible job categories and KSAOs for the cyber workforce,[19] and two used private-sector practices as the basis for possible ratios for information technology (IT) and cyber-personnel relative to the overall workforce.[20] Another insight gleaned from a look at private-sector practices was to manage IT and information or cyber security as distinct career fields.[21] This observation was similar to a recommendation made to the U.S. Air Force in another study focused on military personnel to manage cyberspace operations and cyberwarfare separately, which would facilitate determining required numbers, competencies, and training.[22] Finally, several studies addressed a different type of workforce mix consideration: when to

---

[15] Lindsay Daugherty, Laura Werber, Kristy N. Kamarck, Lisa M. Harrington, and James Gazis, *Officer Accession Planning: A Manual for Estimating Air Force Officer Degree Requirements*, Santa Monica, Calif.: RAND Corporation, TL-196-AF, 2016.

[16] Knopp et al., 2016.

[17] Robson et al., 2020.

[18] Markel et al., 2018.

[19] Paul, Porche, and Axelband, 2014; Porche et al., 2017; Hardison et al., 2019.

[20] Schmidt et al., 2015; Porche et al., 2017.

[21] Schmidt et al., 2015.

[22] Hardison et al., 2019.

rely on knowledge workers not part of the full-time defense workforce. Two studies offered guidance on when to outsource for cyber and data science capabilities while a third presented reserve component personnel as an important part of the cyberworkforce based on their civilian employment pursuits.[23]

While much of the research in this area pertained to cyber, data science, or software personnel, two additional studies looked at different knowledge workers, diversity leaders, and military intelligence analysts. Lytell and her team used a combination of methods, including interviews of DoD leaders and representatives from for-profit organizations, to identify the set of KSAOs that diversity leaders ideally should possess.[24] They include domain-skill knowledge and skills related to equal employment opportunity/military equal opportunity, affirmative action, and diversity; multicultural competence; a commitment to diversity; additional skills less domain specific, such as analytic abilities; and critical thinking and problem-solving skills, interpersonal skills, and leadership skills. In a separate Lytell-directed study,[25] she and her colleagues identified the competencies that Army military intelligence analysts need, which, similar to diversity leaders, included critical thinking and problem-solving skills as well as domain-specific knowledge. They also listed "noncognitive" competency requirements such as adaptability, open-mindedness, and achievement orientation.

A final point of interest regarding requirements for knowledge work that came up in two studies was their malleability, or the degree to which they were modifiable via interventions. For example, in the aforementioned study on diversity leaders,[26] the researchers indicated

---

[23] Schmidt et al., 2015; Knopp et al., 2016; Porche et al., 2017.

[24] Maria C. Lytell, Kirsten M. Keller, Beth Katz, Jefferson P. Marquis, and Jerry M. Sollinger, *Diversity Leadership in the U.S. Department of Defense: Analysis of the Key Roles, Responsibilities, and Attributes of Diversity Leaders*, Santa Monica, Calif.: RAND Corporation, RR-1148-OSD, 2016.

[25] Maria C. Lytell, Susan G. Straus, Chad C. Serena, Geoffrey E. Grimm, James L. Doty III, Jennie W. Wenger, Andrea M. Abler, Andrew M. Naber, Clifford A. Grammich, and Eric S. Fowler, *Assessing Competencies and Proficiency of Army Intelligence Analysts Across the Career Life Cycle*, Santa Monica, Calif.: RAND Corporation, RR-1851-A, 2017.

[26] Lytell et al., 2016.

regarding who performed them—including some plum assignments. Another study suggested that both the perceived lack of a clear vision for the cyberworkforce and insufficient time for technical work as one's career progressed could have a negative influence on recruiting.[33]

The DoD Civilian Acquisition Workforce Personnel Demonstration Project (AcqDemo) was designed to address some of these concerns. For example, its pay-setting flexibilities were intended to position DoD to vie more effectively for highly skilled and highly sought civilian personnel. In its 2016 assessment of AcqDemo,[34] RAND researchers found that supervisors and managers were indeed making use of this flexibility. Starting salaries for individuals who joined DoD's civilian workforce as part of AcqDemo were about $13,000 higher than for comparable personnel who joined DoD's civilian workforce as General Schedule (GS) employees in AcqDemo-eligible organizations. Absent performance data, however, it was unclear whether the flexibility had been used appropriately. In addition, survey results indicate that many supervisors felt that they did not have much discretion to set starting salaries, instead citing impediments such as organization business rules, human resources organizations, and upper management. More generally, supervisors were mixed in their views regarding whether AcqDemo helped with recruiting talent—a contrast with opinions shared by subject-matter experts interviewed as part of this study.

Other studies explored additional strategies to improve DoD recruiting and hiring outcomes. As part of an effort to help the U.S. Air Force make the best use of the Defense Acquisition Workforce Development Fund (DAWDF), Ausink and his team looked at what private-sector companies (including some on the Fortune 100 Best Places to Work list) did to attract talent.[35] Most of the companies represented in

---

[33] Hardison et al., 2019.

[34] Jennifer Lamping Lewis, Laura Werber, Cameron Wright, Irina Danescu, Jessica Hwang, and Lindsay Daugherty, *2016 Assessment of the Civilian Acquisition Workforce Personnel Demonstration Project*, Santa Monica, Calif.: RAND Corporation, RR-1783-OSD, 2017.

[35] John A. Ausink, Lisa M. Harrington, Laura Werber, William A. Williams, Jr., John E. Boon, and Michael H. Powell, *Air Force Management of the Defense Acquisition Workforce Development Fund: Opportunities for Improvement*, Santa Monica, Calif.: RAND Corporation, RR-1486-AF, 2016.

interviews emphasized the usefulness of internship programs in providing a steady supply of high-quality employees. Many of them also cited employee referral bonus programs as a source of promising candidates. Branding—carefully developing, cultivating, and publicizing a specific company image—was also regarded as increasingly important to attract talent. Another strategy increasing in importance was savvy use of social media.

Several studies addressed strategies for recruiting cyberpersonnel, military and civilian. The authors of one study recommended expanding the eligible age range for reserve component recruits to facilitate hiring individuals who work in cyber-related civilian occupations.[36] Other studies encouraged DoD to look beyond technical background for good candidates, which could mean considering candidates who do not hold computer science or engineering degrees or using screening tools to assess not only aptitude but also passion.[37] For example, Schmidt and her colleagues explained that commercial companies gauged passion or affinity through such activities as ethical hacker certifications and participation in open source communities in addition to skills testing focused more on technical expertise.[38] These selection assessments were a complement to formal education requirements but also could be used to vet those without technical degrees. Li and Daugherty's work further attested to the value of cyber-oriented screening tools, particularly to identify those qualified to attain the highest levels of expertise.[39]

Two studies also covered an entirely different approach to obtaining cyberpersonnel: developing them internally rather than hiring them. The National Security Agency was identified as using this approach, at times taking up to three years to develop personnel.[40] In a related vein, many large commercial companies RAND interviewed for another

---

[36] Porche et al., 2017.

[37] Hardison et al., 2019; Schmidt et al., 2015.

[38] Schmidt et al., 2015.

[39] Li and Daugherty, 2015.

[40] Libicki, Senty, and Pollak, 2014.

civilian workforce in the GS system and the subset of those personnel working in AcqDemo eligible organizations not yet part of the demonstration project. Lewis and her colleagues found that AcqDemo participants were more highly educated, more concentrated in technical fields, and more likely to be in a senior-level position than were personnel in either GS-based group.[47]

A few other studies examined the composition of smaller segments of the defense workforce. Markel and his team calculated the size of the security cooperation workforce, which was a difficult endeavor given the distribution of personnel across various DoD, joint, and service organizations.[48] They estimated that the workforce included almost 12,000 U.S civilians, locally hired civilians, military service members, and contractors, with many of them embedded in organizations not expressly focused on security cooperation. Matthews and her coauthors looked at Hispanic representation in DoD's civilian workforce and found that they were underrepresented compared with both the non-DoD federal civilian workforce and the U.S. civilian workforce.[49] Their analysis revealed that some—but not all—of these differences could be explained by differences in education level, citizenship, veteran's status, age, location, and occupation. Lim and his colleagues also looked at Hispanic representation, in this case, their representation among those holding a STEM degree and those in the STEM workforce.[50] They found that Hispanics constituted 20 percent of the overall young adult population (ages 23–29) but just 7 percent of those with degrees in STEM fields and only 5 percent of those with a college degree who work in STEM occupations. Comparable figures for the Black young adult population were 13 percent of the overall population, 6 percent of those with degrees in STEM fields, and 4 percent of professionals with college degrees employed in STEM occupations. Additional analysis that compared the overall STEM civilian work-

[47] Lewis et al., 2017.

[48] Markel et al., 2018.

[49] Matthews et al., 2017.

[50] Lim et al., 2013.

force and DoD civilian STEM workforce using a definition of STEM that included health practitioners showed that the DoD civilian STEM workforce has a slightly higher Black population (10 percent and 8 percent, respectively) and comparable Hispanic populations (5 percent and 6 percent, respectively).[51] These racial and ethnic differences were partly explained by differences in educational attainment.

Turning their attention to gender differences, Lim and his colleagues determined that women were also significantly underrepresented in STEM fields compared with their proportion in the overall young adult population (49 percent of young adult population, 40 percent of young adults with STEM degrees, 31 percent of young adults in STEM occupations).[52] Using the definition of STEM that included health practitioners, Lim and his colleagues found that the overall STEM workforce was 51 percent female, while the DoD civilian STEM workforce was only 29 percent female. In contrast with the racial and ethnic results, the gender gaps in STEM outcomes were not explained by differences in overall educational attainment because women were more likely to hold college degrees.

In a later study, Schulker and Matthews looked more closely at women's representation in the overall DoD workforce (i.e., not only the DoD STEM workforce) and found that women were underrepresented in the DoD civilian workforce relative to both the non-DoD federal civilian workforce and the U.S. civilian labor force.[53] They also determined that the proportion of employees who were veterans was the main contributor to the explained portion of these gaps.

Veteran status also was an explanatory factor for differences between the DoD and non-DoD federal workforce in terms of the proportion of people with disabilities in each. Whether people with disabilities were under- or overrepresented in DoD depended in part

---

[51] The authors explained that these calculations included health practitioners in their definition of STEM to match the DoD definition of STEM occupations.

[52] Lim et al., 2013.

[53] David Schulker and Miriam Matthews, *Women's Representation in the U.S. Department of Defense Workforce: Addressing the Influence of Veterans' Employment*, Santa Monica, Calif.: RAND Corporation, RR-2458-OSD, 2018.

on the definition of disability status used. For example, for PWTD, DoD representation is lower than both the level in the non-DoD federal workforce and the 2-percent federal representation goals. But since DoD has a considerably higher representation of veterans with at least a 30-percent disability rating than other federal agencies, comparisons including that group show relatively high disability representation in DoD.[54]

---

[54] Matthews et al., 2018.

CHAPTER FOUR

Train and Develop

Many of the studies included in this review either were expressly focused on T&D issues or touched on these aspects of talent management as part of a broader effort. In this section I present three sets of findings related to T&D: those focused on a particular segment of knowledge workers, those related to education opportunities available from the private sector, and those pertaining to assessment and evaluation.

Training and Development for Specific Types of Knowledge Workers

T&D for three types of knowledge workers—cyber- or IT professionals, data scientists, and supervisors—appear to be of interest to DoD based on RAND publications. That was particularly the case for cyber-professionals, whose training was considered in multiple studies. Two studies reported that providing regular training to sustain or deepen technical expertise was especially critical for the cyberworkforce, notably cyberofficers and those in manager roles.[1] Looking to the private sector for insights on how this type of training is accomplished, Schmidt and her team found that commercial firms allow managers to specialize to some degree so that there are fewer technological trends and changes on which they need to keep current.[2] These firms also use

---

[1] Hardison et al., 2019; Schmidt et al., 2015.

[2] Schmidt et al., 2015.

standards to use in performance rating. At the time of the study, DoD had taken some but not all of those actions.

Learning from the Private Sector

The role of the private sector in providing educational opportunities to DoD personnel was a common topic in the studies I reviewed. Such opportunities include T&D offered by external (non-DoD) colleges and universities as well as such educational resources as professional certifications and industry-based internships. In one of the earlier studies included in this review, Libicki, Senty, and Pollak reported that the National Security Agency had designated three universities not run by DoD as Centers of Academic Excellence in Cyber Operations.[7] As of this writing in 2020, the number of such centers had grown considerably, and there are also Centers of Academic Excellence for Cyber Defense Education.[8] In a related vein, Li and Daugherty noted that defense agencies were taking advantage of many college- and university-based language programs for their personnel and DoD-established partnerships, including the Language Flagship, Project GO, and the Language Training Centers.[9] Werber and her coauthors found that a small number of defense acquisition personnel were participating in short university-run courses to gain knowledge of industry.[10] In addition, Robson and his colleagues suggested that civilian education providers could also help defense personnel acquire the software competencies they need, particularly for competencies that are not DoD specific.[11]

---

[7] Libicki, Senty, and Pollak, 2014.

[8] Information about current Centers of Academy Excellence in Cyber Operations and Cyber Defense Education is available at National Security Agency Central Security Service, "National Centers of Academic Excellence in Cybersecurity," webpage, undated.

[9] Li and Daugherty, 2015.

[10] Werber et al., 2019.

[11] Robson et al., 2020.

Looking beyond colleges and universities, Porche and his coauthors cross-walked major civilian certifications with over 900 cyber-mission force knowledge, skills, and abilities (KSAs) and found that most of those certifications covered the majority of those KSAs.[12] Professional certifications were also regarded as a possible means of conferring various types of knowledge of industry, but the subject-matter experts they interviewed were of mixed opinions regarding their suitability.[13] In the same study, subject-matter experts viewed internships or rotations with industry as a productive way to gain knowledge of industry. Robson and his team also raised the possibility of using massive open online courses (e.g., Coursera) as a way to provide software-related training.[14]

More often than not, private-sector T&D options were discussed in a favorable way as a possible complement or alternative to DoD-provided education. As noted above, however, professional certifications were not always a well-regarded substitute for DoD-based learning assets.[15] The value of other options was limited for a different reason: capacity constraints. For example, the number of personnel participating in industry rotations or "knowledge of industry" executive-education-type courses in any given year was very small.[16] Finally, as I discuss in the next section, although DoD efforts to evaluate T&D have been limited, Li and Daugherty reported that with the exception of Language Flagship universities and a few others, most university-based language training was regarded as falling short of DoD requirements in some way.[17]

---

[12] Porche et al., 2017.

[13] Werber et al., 2019.

[14] Robson et al., 2020.

[15] Robson et al., 2020.

[16] Robson et al., 2020.

[17] Li and Daugherty, 2015.

Assessment and Evaluation

Several studies identified problems that DoD has with respect to assessing its training needs and to evaluating the effectiveness of its personnel's T&D activities. In their study of potential gaps in knowledge of industry present within the defense acquisition workforce, Werber and her coauthors noted that the lack of clarity on the type of knowledge required and the desired proficiency level made it difficult either to assess the extent to which gaps existed or to determine the T&D that would best confer the necessary knowledge.[18] They also found that the timing and methods that DoD uses to assess defense acquisition workforce proficiency varied greatly, further stymieing efforts to identify gaps. Robson and his colleagues made similar observations with respect to software competency gaps.[19] They advised DoD to identify the importance of each desired software competency and check for competency gaps before determining what T&D resources were needed. In addition to the challenges related to understanding training needs and proficiency levels noted above, insufficient evaluation of various T&D initiatives has been a persistent concern over the years as well. Ausink and colleagues noted that although the DAWDF charter requires the Directors of Acquisition Career Management (commonly referred to as "DACMs") to develop measurable objectives for funded proposals and to use metrics to track their performance, the U.S. Air Force and other military services have struggled to meet those requirements.[20] In the study mentioned above about gaps in knowledge of industry presented within the defense acquisition workforce, Werber and her colleagues also reported that although DoD uses surveys to obtain feedback from Defense Acquisition University students and, for some classes, their supervisors as well, overall DoD efforts to evaluate T&D, particularly options offered by external (non-DoD) providers, were inconsistent and limited.[21] Moreover, the methods used to gauge

---

[18] Werber et al., 2019.

[19] Robson et al., 2020.

[20] Ausink et al., 2016.

[21] Werber et al., 2019.

effectiveness were inadequate, focused primarily on reactions and learning and less on outcomes. In a look at training for DoD supervisors, researchers found that desired training outcomes were not always clear, and outcome measures were limited—both of which presented barriers to evaluation.[22]

On a more positive note, three studies included specific measures that could be used to gauge proficiency and consequently to evaluate T&D effectiveness. Although the studies were focused on a specific model, program, or job series, some of the measures may be useful for knowledge work more broadly. For example, as part of the Straus-led study about the leadership attributes included in ALRM, the team identified tools to measure psychological constructs that map on to those attributes.[23] For example, ALRM includes five attributes related to intellect—mental agility, sound judgment, innovation, interpersonal tact, and expertise—and for each of those attributes, the researchers identified constructs that correspond with each attribute (e.g., creative problem solving for innovation) and commonly used, scientifically validated measures for each. They also offer guidelines on the use of such measures. In a different Straus-led study that evaluated the effectiveness of the Army's Asymmetric Warfare Adaptive Leader Program—a program intended to promote adaptability in military leaders and to facilitate innovative thinking related to unified land operations—the researchers offer other ways to evaluate T&D that they indicated may be applicable to other T&D activities.[24] Their report features a set of instruments, tools, and protocols that can be used to measure adaptability and possibly to evaluate other T&D modalities intended to enhance intangible skills (e.g., teamwork, leadership skills) that seem especially important for knowledge work. Finally, the Lytell and colleagues study on key competencies for Army military intelligence analysts lists spe-

---

[22] Werber et al., 2018.

[23] Straus et al., 2018.

[24] Susan G. Straus, Michael G. Shanley, Carra S. Sims, Bryan W. Hallmark, Anna Rosefsky Saavedra, Stoney Trent, and Sean Duggan, *Innovative Leader Development: Evaluation of the U.S. Army Asymmetric Warfare Adaptive Leader Program*, Santa Monica, Calif.: RAND Corporation, RR-504-A, 2014.

cific ways to measure those competencies, including validated instruments, standardized tests, writing sample reviews, and interviews.[25] For example, the Watson-Glaser Critical Thinking Appraisal is a way to assess critical thinking skills and by extension T&D intended to improve those skills. Another instrument they cited was the Tailored Adaptive Personality Assessment System, which measures constructs such as open-mindedness and conscientiousness. In a related vein, Li and Daugherty presented evaluation practices from the defense language field that could be applied to other contexts.[26] They described the field's shared definitions and metrics. In particular, the Interagency Language Roundtable scale and skill-level descriptions were perceived as providing those who deliver training, assess skills, and employ defense language professionals a common understanding of training objectives and outcomes.

---

[25] Lytell et al., 2017.

[26] Li and Daugherty, 2015.

CHAPTER FIVE

Motivate and Manage Performance

In this section, I highlight research findings intended to help DoD to sustain or improve performance of its civilian employees, knowledge workers in particular. They cover financial incentives, nonfinancial incentives, and other strategies for maximizing employee performance. As Ross and her colleagues noted in their study on the STEM workforce, "Both extrinsic and intrinsic rewards can significantly boost STEM workers' productivity. When properly implemented, rewards and recognition help strengthen STEM employees' efficiency and motivation."[1]

Financial Incentives

The bulk of findings related to financial incentives are from Lewis and her coauthors' 2016 assessment of AcqDemo.[2] Within AcqDemo, the authors found that both raises and awards are linked to individual performance (referred to as "contribution" within AcqDemo) as intended. They also determined, however, that female and nonwhite employees had slower salary growth than their counterparts in the GS system. In addition, although higher levels of contribution were associated with

---

[1] Shirley M. Ross, Rebecca Herman, Irina A. Chindea, Samantha E. Dinicola, and Amy Grace Donohue, *Optimizing the Contributions of Air Force Civilian STEM Workforce*, Santa Monica, Calif.: RAND Corporation, RR-4234-AF, 2020, p. ix.

[2] Lewis et al., 2017.

higher salaries, a survey of AcqDemo participants revealed that most AcqDemo employees did not believe that a link between contribution and compensation existed. This perception could have diminished the ability of raises to incentivize a higher level of effort. Similarly, AcqDemo's one-time awards for notable contributions were perhaps less effective than they could have been because most of the organizations under AcqDemo opted to give smaller awards to a large number of employees rather than large amounts to an exceptional few. Specifically, the study team estimated that during the FY 2015 review cycle, 92 percent of AcqDemo participants received a contribution award, and the bulk of them received an award totaling less than $2,000. This almost-universal availability of awards could have further reduced the perceived link between contribution and compensation and the award's power as an incentive.

Ausink and his team considered the value of financial incentives but from a different angle: they looked for lessons from the private sector.[3] They found that many companies, both the Fortune 100 Best Places to Work companies represented in interviews and in the U.S. workplace more generally, use spot bonuses and awards to acknowledge exceptional employee performance. Such merit-based awards vary not only in terms of their formality but also in terms of who does the recognition. More formal programs may involve a nomination process, selection committee, and organizationwide recognition, while less formal options use low-value awards to recognize going above and beyond closer to real time. Some companies also provide ways for employees to recognize their peers with small cash awards, in some cases, even without requiring leader approval. The researchers also reported that some organizations amplify the incentive value of these programs by promoting them internally, such as via a newsfeed or intranet website.

Another widely used incentive that RAND identified in the same study was tuition assistance. Ausink and his colleagues emphasized that companies varied widely in how they implemented this incen-

---

[3]   Ausink et al., 2016.

tive, however.[4] They differed in terms of employee eligibility, dollar amounts, employment obligations following the coursework, acceptable degrees, and grade requirements. Based on the team's interviews with representatives of companies on the Fortune 100 Best Places to Work list, tailoring this employee benefit to align with the company's human capital strategy was key.

Nonfinancial Incentives

Two studies explored nonpecuniary ways that DoD could motivate and reward its employees, focusing on the acquisition workforce and STEM workforce.[5] Ausink and his team found that some organizations have merit award programs that use highly visible recognition as an incentive rather than a financial benefit.[6] More compelling, however, was the perceived incentive value of challenging, meaningful work. Interviewees from Fortune 100 Best Places to Work organizations discussed the importance of engaging work to motivating and retaining employees and indicated it was entwined with employee development. They explained that tuition assistance was appealing not only due to its financial value but also as a means of engaging employees with continuous learning. More generally, lifelong learning via educational opportunities—such as coursework (in-house or external), skill-extending job assignments, and lateral job transfers—was viewed as a means to attract, motivate, and retain employees. Ross and her colleagues' work included similar findings.[7] Specifically, their literature review indicated that professional growth is a strong motivator for STEM employees. By providing opportunities for such growth, DoD and other organizations can positively influence those employees' intrinsic motivation.

---

[4] Ausink et al., 2016.

[5] Ausink et al., 2016; Ross et al., 2020.

[6] Ausink et al., 2016.

[7] Ausink et al., 2016.

Additional Strategies to Sustain or Improve Performance

Several studies included descriptions of organizational practices or structures that could promote strong employee performance. Two focused on different performance feedback processes. Hardison and her colleagues assessed whether 360-degree reviews (360s)—in which personnel receive feedback from supervisors, subordinates, and peers—would be useful in military settings.[8] They considered the advantages and disadvantages of 360s for both evaluative and developmental purposes. Based on their research within and outside the military context, the researchers recommended *not* using 360s for officer evaluations, but they did see merit in using 360s in a targeted way, to develop individuals in higher grades or leadership positions. As part of another project on support for DoD supervisors with poor performing employees,[9] Werber and her team identified increased use of ongoing check-ins as a helpful way to nip performance concerns in the bud rather than waiting for an annual review to address them. In addition, they found that some organizations used high-tech tools to facilitate those regular check-ins. Such tools further supported supervisors by making it easy for them to capture and store performance information in an ongoing way and guiding them through the steps recommended to handle poor performance. These tools were regarded as a supplement to the supervisor training discussed earlier in this report.

Affinity groups (also referred to as employee resource groups) were identified as another way to cultivate good performance, particularly for women and minority groups. Ausink and his coauthors focused on the learning, networking, and mentoring opportunities that such programs provide.[10] Matthews and her team discussed another potential benefit of affinity groups: creating an inclusive, welcoming envi-

---

[8]   Chaitra M. Hardison, Mikhail Zaydman, Tobi A. Oluwatola, Anna Rosefsky Saavedra, Thomas Bush, Heather Peterson, and Susan G. Straus, *360-Degree Assessments: Are They the Right Tool for the U.S. Military?*, Santa Monica, Calif.: RAND Corporation, RR-998-OSD, 2015.

[9]   Werber et al., 2018.

[10] Ausink et al., 2016.

ronment that provides a supportive context for minority employees—
in their study, Hispanic employees—to thrive.[11] To increase affinity
groups' credibility and effectiveness, they recommended senior level support and endorsement.

Finally, two studies described how organizational structure, decentralized structures in particular, could have a positive effect on employee
performance. Schmidt and her colleagues reported that commercial
organizations tended to use a more decentralized structure for their
information security function, particularly compared with their IT function.[12] Information security organizations largely consisted of small,
cross-functional teams, and leaders pushed decisionmaking down to
the employee level to the greatest extent possible to facilitate rapid
responses, which often were required. In a related vein, Ross and her
team[13] extolled the virtues of the decentralized organization, with a
simplified or even flat structure and autonomous teams, for the STEM
workforce. Their research indicated that such a structure would likely
promote innovation and could help performance more generally by
fostering knowledge sharing and collaboration across the workforce.

---

[11] Matthews et al., 2017.

[12] Schmidt et al., 2015.

[13] Ross et al., 2020.

CHAPTER SIX

Promote and Retain the Right Talent

This section features findings related to promotion outcomes, retention outcomes, and policies and strategies that may influence retention. Overall, they provide insights about the extent to which DoD is promoting and retaining knowledge workers and other DoD personnel and suggest actions the department can take to ensure it is promoting and retaining the right talent.

Characteristics of Those Promoted

Promoting high performers at a higher rate than other personnel seems intuitive. It is difficult to assess, however, the degree to which this happens in DoD due to the quality of its performance data. Focusing on the defense acquisition workforce, documented performance tends to be limited to supervisor ratings of individual performance. Moreover, standardized performance ratings in Defense Manpower Data Center files are lacking in detail and variance. To this second point, as part of the 2016 AcqDemo assessment,[1] Lewis and her team reported that only about half of permanent, full-time GS employees were rated on the full five-point scale. The majority of the remainder was graded as either "fully successful" or "unsatisfactory"—essentially a pass/fail scale. Of those rated on the five-point scale, less than 1 percent received the two lowest ratings of 1 ("unsatisfactory") or 2 ("minimally satisfactory").

---

[1] Lewis et al., 2017.

An earlier study by Guo, Hall-Partyka, and Gates also found that use of the five-point scale was limited and in application tended to be only a three-point scale (less than 1 percent of employees on the "H" performance plan received a 1 or 2).[2] Lewis and her colleagues were able to work around these limitations by using more detailed performance ratings data maintained by the AcqDemo Program Office. Specifically, they found that by a small but statistically significant margin, employees with higher contribution scores were more likely to be promoted than were employees with low contribution score.

Other findings about who was promoted pertain to characteristics other than performance, such as gender, race, ethnicity, and organizational membership. Turning our attention first to gender, Lewis and her team found that women in AcqDemo experienced fewer promotions compared with their counterparts in the GS system. In their analysis of promotions to the Senior Executive Service (SES)—arguably an elite group of knowledge workers—Guo, Hall-Partyka, and Gates reported that gender was not a significant predictor of whether an employee was promoted to SES.[3] They suggested this outcome was due in part to women tending to work in career fields that are underrepresented in SES. For example, during the time frame of this analysis, over 50 percent of SES were from the systems engineering career field, but only 8 percent of women in the acquisition workforce work in systems engineering, compared with 34 percent of men.

Looking at race and ethnicity, in their AcqDemo assessment, Lewis and her team determined that nonwhite employees, 59 percent of whom were Black, experienced fewer promotions than their equivalents in the GS system.[4] Within AcqDemo, after controlling for other factors, there were no differences in promotion rates between white

---

[2]   Christopher Guo, Philip Hall-Partyka, and Susan M. Gates, *Retention and Promotion of High-Quality Civil Service Workers in the Department of Defense Acquisition Workforce*, Santa Monica, Calif.: RAND Corporation, RR-748-OSD, 2014.

[3]   Guo, Hall-Partyka, and Gates, 2014.

[4]   Lewis et al., 2017. Due to the small size of the sample, the study authors were not able to obtain a reliable estimate of the promotion difference between Black employees in AcqDemo and comparable Black employees in the GS system.

employees and Black employees, white employees and Asian employees, or non-Hispanic and Hispanic employees. Guo, Hall-Partyka, and Gates reported that race was not a significant predictor of promotion to SES and again cited underrepresentation in career fields that have a disproportionate number of SES as a reason. In a third study that looked at the DoD workforce overall,[5] the authors found that Hispanics tended to work in occupations with lower rates of promotion, and those who do work in high-promoting occupations are less likely to be promoted than non-Hispanic employees.

The analysis of factors related to promotion to SES also revealed some organization characteristics that play a role.[6] Specifically, relative to their representation in the acquisition workforce, individuals with a U.S. Army background are overrepresented in SES, and individuals with an Office of the Secretary of Defense background are underrepresented in SES. Compared with members of the baseline career field of systems engineering, members of the program management, auditing, and production quality career fields were more likely to join the SES ranks, and those in the business career field were less likely.

Characteristics of Those Retained

Similar to the preceding section, I start with findings related to performance and then summarize those related to individual and organizational characteristics. The Guo-led study and separate Lewis-led study covered earlier in the discussion of promotions also include insights related to retention. Working with the less detailed performance ratings data available for the entire defense acquisition workforce, Guo, Hall-Partyka, and Gates determined that higher average performance ratings were associated with an increased hazard of separation (i.e., lower likelihood of retention) within the acquisition workforce, especially higher-grade employees.[7] Comparable results were

---

[5] Matthews et al., 2017.

[6] Guo, Hall-Partyka, and Gates, 2014.

[7] Guo, Hall-Partyka, and Gates, 2014.

obtained when different indicators of performance (e.g., initial performance ratings) were included in their statistical models.[8] A few years later and using different performance ratings (provided by AcqDemo), Lewis and her team's analysis indicated that within AcqDemo, high-performing employees (based on overall contribution score) were more likely to be retained than were low-performing employees.[9]

Research indicated that other individual-level characteristics also appear to be related to retention, although whether the right talent is being retained is less clear. Guo, Hall-Partyka, and Gates considered what they regarded to be an additional indicator of performance quality—education—in their analysis of retention. In statistical models that included final education level, members of the acquisition workforce with a bachelor's or graduate degree were more likely to be retained than those with less than a bachelor's degree.[10] As part of the AcqDemo assessment, however, researchers found that education level did not have a statistically significant relationship with retention outcomes when performance ratings and other individual and organizational characteristics were taken into account.[11]

With an eye toward cultivating and retaining a diverse workforce, two studies indicated that women were retained at lower rates than men within DoD. Lewis and her colleagues found that within AcqDemo, women were retained at lower rates than men, but they also noted that was true of the equivalent GS population.[12] A couple of years later, Schulker and Matthews came to a similar conclusion in their analysis of the DoD civilian workforce.[13] Lewis and her team also reported that Black and Asian employees fared well within AcqDemo: they were retained at higher rates within AcqDemo than their white counterparts. In contrast, Hispanic participants in AcqDemo were retained at

---

[8]   Guo, Hall-Partyka, and Gates, 2014.

[9]   Lewis et al., 2017.

[10]   Guo, Hall-Partyka, and Gates, 2014.

[11]   Lewis et al., 2017.

[12]   Lewis et al., 2017.

[13]   Schulker and Matthews, 2018.

lower rates than their non-Hispanic counterparts. Matthews and her colleagues also noted a different type of retention issue related to Hispanic members of DoD's civilian workforce: they constituted a larger percentage of separations than new hires, especially in the U.S. Air Force and DoD fourth estate agencies.[14]

The last set of retention factors pertains to organizational membership. Gates and her team reported that attrition was not only low in the civilian defense acquisition workforce in an absolute sense (5.1 to 5.6 percent versus 7.8 to 8.6 percent) but also lower relative to the DoD civilian workforce overall.[15] They also noted retention differences by career field; most notably members of the contracting career field were retained at a lower rate rather than the acquisition workforce overall, and members of the engineering career field were retained at a higher rate. Several studies also hinted at problems related to retaining cyberpersonnel but did not provide precise attrition rates or retention comparisons.[16] Finally, Guo, Hall-Partyka, and Gates presented evidence that civilians who entered the acquisition workforce and were part of a demonstration pay plan (e.g., AcqDemo, Science and Technology Reinvention Laboratory Demonstration Program) were retained longer than those under the GS plan.[17] Their analysis indicated that compared with the GS plan, retention increased by 18 percent for the AcqDemo pay plan and by 12 percent for other demonstration plans.

Policy and Strategy Influences on Retention

Actions that may help or hinder DoD in retaining the right talent were a popular research topic. Several studies addressed how compensation may influence retention. Asch, Mattock, and Hosek used an economic

---

[14] Matthews et al., 2017.

[15] Gates et al., 2018.

[16] Hardison et al., 2019; Porche et al., 2017; Jennie W. Wenger, Caolionn O'Connell, and Maria C. Lytell, *Retaining the Army's Cyber Expertise*, Santa Monica, Calif.: RAND Corporation, RR-1978-A, 2017.

[17] Guo, Hall-Partyka, and Gates, 2014.

model along with 24 years of data on federal civil service employment to simulate the effects of unpaid furloughs and pay freezes on DoD civilian workforce retention.[18] They simulated the effect of an unpaid six-day furlough, which is what federal employees experienced in 2013 due to sequestration, and found that it had no apparent effect on retention for either the GS workforce overall or the GS STEM workforce in particular. In contrast, their models indicated that uncertainty over the length of a pay freeze can have a potentially large effect on both the overall GS workforce and the GS STEM workforce even if personnel are confident that pay will be restored within ten years. This finding was somewhat surprising since, as Asch, Mattock, and Hosek explained in their report, civilian personnel have a positive taste for defense employment and tend to stay because they value nonfinancial aspects of the work, such as job security, stability, and work in the public interest.

Other studies looked to the private sector for insights about the influence of compensation on retention. In their study about cyber-related lessons from commercial firms, Schmidt and her colleagues found that high salaries were not regarded as the primary influence on retention.[19] In fact, they determined that median salaries for corporate IT and information security professionals were similar to the pay and benefits that military personnel receive when additional allowances and tax advantages are taken into account. Ausink and his team also considered the private sector in their work and reported that retention bonuses were not a widely used retention tool either by the Fortune 100 Best Places to Work companies represented in interviews or by the private sector in general.[20] Interviewees tended to view them as a last resort.

Similar to performance, some strategies to incentivize personnel to stay were not based on financial compensation. Many of the prac-

[18] Beth J. Asch, Michael G. Mattock, and James Hosek, *The Federal Civil Service Workforce: Assessing the Effects on Retention of Pay Freezes, Unpaid Furloughs, and Other Federal-Employee Compensation Changes in the Department of Defense*, Santa Monica, Calif.: RAND Corporation, RR-514-OSD, 2014.

[19] Schmidt et al., 2015.

[20] Ausink et al., 2016.

tices cited as motivating individuals to perform at a higher level were also identified as helping to retain talent. They include meaningful, challenging work;[21] ample career development opportunities in the form of education or promotions;[22] mentoring;[23] and affinity groups.[24]

The last two strategies intended to help DoD retain the right talent were of a different ilk. First, the Ausink-led team stressed the value of DAWDF as a basis for funding retention initiatives, particularly novel ideas that could benefit from pilot testing or those intended for a specific segment of the workforce.[25] In their report, they presented a framework for evaluating proposals to ensure DAWDF is used strategically and offered other suggestions to improve DAWDF use, such as greater process transparency and clear metrics to assess the performance of initiatives that are selected for funding. Werber and her colleagues looked at retaining the right talent from a different angle: they focused on the problem of poor-performing civilian employees and noted that supervisors neither consistently nor effectively used policies and procedures, such as probationary periods, performance improvement plans, or legal authorities governing employee dismissals.[26] The study team identified actions DoD could take to improve the use of these tools, including enhancing its email notification capabilities to advise supervisors about the timing of their subordinates' probationary periods and involving HR professionals as early as possible when poor performance is noted so that supervisors are supported as they navigate what can be a complex process.

---

[21] Asch, Mattock, and Hosek, 2014; Ausink et al., 2016; Schmidt et al., 2015.

[22] Ausink et al., 2016; Hardison et al., 2019; Guo, Hall-Partyka, and Gates, 2014; Ross et al., 2020; Schmidt et al., 2015.

[23] Matthews et al., 2017.

[24] Ausink et al., 2016; Matthews et al., 2017.

[25] Ausink et al., 2016.

[26] Werber et al., 2018.

CHAPTER SEVEN

Data Issues Present Challenges to Effective Talent Management

Data-related shortcomings were a persistent theme that cut across all aspects of talent management. DoD's data systems were the main focus of one study, which pertained to DoD workforce supply and demand analysis. Nataraj and her colleagues explained that in most cases, personnel data (i.e., "faces") and manpower data (i.e., "spaces," or authorizations) were maintained in separate systems.[1] This disconnect made it difficult to identify when positions are not filled. They also noted problems that could affect DoD efforts to build and organize its workforce. For example, since civilians and contractors were managed locally rather than centrally, civilian requirements data were not authoritative, and contractor authorizations data were limited. In addition, there were data disconnects related to occupations, which makes occupation-specific analysis challenging. Manpower analysts tend to think about functions or activities rather than occupations, for instance, and some workforce segments could not be easily identified by occupation codes. These segments included groups of knowledge workers, such as members of the acquisition workforce and the cyber-workforce. Robson and his team noted a similar problem with respect to software.[2] At the time of their research, DoD did not have a system

---

[1] Shanthi Nataraj, Christopher Guo, Philip Hall-Partyka, Susan M. Gates, and Douglas Yeung, *Options for Department of Defense Total Workforce Supply and Demand Analysis: Potential Approaches and Available Data Sources*, Santa Monica, Calif.: RAND Corporation, RR-543-OSD, 2014.

[2] Robson et al., 2020.

for identifying or tracking who carries out software functions. This lack of a system appeared to be a problem for data science as well, at least at DIA, where Knopp and his colleagues found that individuals using data science techniques were neither labeled nor tracked as such.[3]

A few studies touched on data shortcomings related to hiring. Matthews and her team demonstrated the value of analyzing job applicant data but also noted limitations, such as many applications not including ethnicity information and USAJOBS data in particular lacking information on the status of applications at any stage of the hiring process.[4] In a different study, Matthews and her coauthors suggested that veterans may be underreporting targeted disabilities, which would make it more difficult for DoD to monitor how well individuals with targeted disabilities were represented in either its applicant pool or its workforce.[5] Hardison and her colleagues also discussed the usefulness of collecting additional characteristics about applicants for cyberpositions and those ultimately selected for those positions.[6] They also recommended collecting perceptions about the job at various points in one's career, starting at the applicant stage, which would help with developing strategies to market cybercareer opportunities to highpotential prospects, determining whether the right people were being recruited, and managing new hires' expectations.

Researchers also identified several data challenges related to tracking T&D experiences. In their report on the U.S. Army's cybercapabilities, Porche and his coauthors explained that the U.S. Army's awareness of the cyberskills present within the reserve component was hindered by the dwindling response rate for the Civilian Employment Information database, which personnel were supposed to update annually.[7] They encouraged DoD to not only find a way to increase compliance but also suggested adding items to collect more detail on cyber-

---

[3] Knopp et al., 2016.

[4] Matthews et al., 2017.

[5] Matthews et al., 2018.

[6] Hardison et al., 2019.

[7] Porche et al., 2017.

related skills. Werber and her colleagues reported the DoD did not have a good understanding of who may have knowledge of industry because its tracking of activities that may confer this type of knowledge was limited.[8] For example, DoD centralized personnel databases lacked information about the type of graduate degrees held by defense acquisition personnel (e.g., the department could not readily ascertain who or how many personnel have a master of business administration), and individual personnel records did not typically capture all T&D activities. In addition, industry rotations and fellowships were tracked separately and differently by the military services. The resultant lack of clarity rendered it difficult to identify people most in need of specific developmental activities and has prevented DoD from reporting the required metrics related to industry-based training.

Motivating and managing performance was also impeded by data issues. In their assessment of AcqDemo, Lewis and her colleagues identified problems related to GS system performance ratings.[9] As mentioned earlier in this report, although the GS system had a five-point ratings scale, Lewis and her team found that only about half of permanent, full-time GS employees were rated on the full scale. The majority of the remainder was evaluated using a pass/fail scale. In addition, the researchers reported that performance ratings within the GS system and within AcqDemo appeared to have experienced inflation over time. Other data problems with implications for performance management pertained to poor-performing employees. Werber and her coauthors learned that one of DoD's personnel management databases, the Defense Civilian Personnel Data System, did not always have accurate information about employees' first-line supervisor.[10] At the time of their study, this information had to be input manually into the system. This limitation meant that DoD could not readily notify supervisors that an employee's probationary period was soon ending and prompt them to consider whether that employment relationship should continue. Also regarding poor-performing civilian employees,

---

[8] Werber et al., 2019.

[9] Lewis et al., 2017.

[10] Werber et al., 2018.

the study team found that tracking of poor performers and actions taken to address their performance (e.g., developing a performance improvement plan) was decentralized, with metrics that varied in terms of both type and timing. This situation made it challenging for DoD component heads to monitor how consistently and how well poor performance was addressed across their organization and again hampered DoD's ability to report required metrics, in this case those listed in Executive Order 13839, *Promoting Accountability and Streamlining Removal Procedures Consistent with Merit System Principles*.

Finally, references to data issues that could affect promoting and retaining the right talent were relatively limited. Some of the observations noted earlier apply here as well—for example, insufficient coding of occupations and tracking of those performing software and data science functions can make it difficult to follow the career trajectories of specific types of knowledge workers and to evaluate whether targeted strategies are needed to retain them in sufficient number. Other studies mentioned the infrequent use of exit surveys and interviews, which were seen as a potentially rich source of information that could identify concerns important for DoD to address and help evaluate the value of retention strategies.[11]

---

[11] See, for example, Hardison et al., 2019.

Conclusion

Overall, RAND research has much to tell policymakers and analysts about knowledge worker talent management. Findings span the full cycle of talent management, including the four pillars of talent management described at the start of this report:

- build and organize
- train and develop
- motivate and manage performance
- promote and retain the right talent.

Some studies focused on a specific segment of knowledge workers, most frequently those with cyberskills but also those working in data science or software, STEM professionals, defense acquisition personnel, military intelligence analysts, supervisors, diversity leaders, and military leaders. Findings related to diversity management cut across the four pillars as well, with studies featuring observations related to recruitment, development, and/or retention of such groups as women, racial and ethnic minorities, and PWTD. In many cases, researchers identified problems DoD was experiencing or areas in need of improvement, but they offered solutions to those concerns and identified ways for DoD to adopt a proactive approach to talent management. Although some studies were focused on military personnel performing knowledge work, such as military intelligence analysts and Army leaders responsible for unified land operations and others (such as the two about the AcqDemo personnel demonstration project) clearly pertained to civilian personnel, in many cases, study findings could apply to either category of defense knowledge workers. For example, measures to gauge proficiency in such attributes as adaptability, critical thinking, and creative problem solving could be used to evaluate T&D for either type of personnel, and such practices as meaningful work, opportunities for lifelong learning, and decentralized organizational structure may appeal to—and be feasible for—military and civilian knowledge workers alike.

The body of work included in this review also highlighted tools or policy levers DoD already has, insights from the private sector for DoD to consider, and a wide array of tools developed or identified by RAND that DoD can use to improve how it manages knowledge workers. AcqDemo has many features intended to help attract, reward, and retain top talent, but they may not be used to their full extent. For example, supervisors felt their ability to set starting salaries was limited, and they were not making full use of that flexibility. Similarly, although AcqDemo was successful in retaining high contributors at a higher rate than low contributors, giving small awards to many personnel versus large awards to a smaller group of top performers could diminish the perceived link between contribution and pay. In addition, DAWDF is available to fund recruiting and retention initiatives, but transparency regarding how initiatives are selected and evaluated to ensure they are achieving their intended outcomes were both lacking.

The private sector was a source of promising ideas related to several aspects of talent management. Research on commercial firms showed they try to gauge passion in addition to technical expertise when evaluating cyberjob candidates and provided information about how they manage IT and cyber career fields and develop personnel working therein. Internships, employee referral bonuses, branding, and the deliberate use of social media were popular approaches to attract talent for companies on the Fortune 100 Best Places to Work list. Moreover, private-sector firms' strategic use of tuition assistance, merit awards of varying monetary value and prestige, engagement of employees via challenging developmental opportunities and meaningful work, affinity groups, and decentralized organizational structure were cited in various studies as ways to attract, motivate, and/or retain knowledge workers. Finally, some researchers suggested that the private-sector organizations, at times along with public-sector providers, may be a source of T&D activities that could complement or in some cases substitute for DoD-based T&D assets. Such opportunities include internships with industry, offerings from colleges and universities, massive open online courses, and professional certifications. Not all these practices and resources may easily transfer to the DoD context (e.g., employee referral bonuses may not be applicable in a civil service context), but others present opportunities for innovation and experimentation within DoD that warrant additional attention.

Taken together, the reviewed studies also include many resources developed or identified by RAND researchers that can help DoD to improve its capacity for knowledge worker talent management. For example, as part of efforts that fall under the build and organize pillar, researchers constructed a definition of STEM and wrote a manual to help estimate STEM degree requirements, identified key competencies or KSAOs for several types of knowledge workers, drafted position descriptions for data science specialties, identified job families and competencies for security cooperation, and built a software competency model for DoD to validate. Other studies' work products include a training structure framework, a framework for evaluating proposals submitted for DAWDF support, and instruments, tools, and protocols that can be used to measure proficiency in different attributes important to knowledge work and to evaluate T&D activities intended to cultivate them. This review also revealed gaps in RAND's DoD-sponsored research, at least among studies cleared for public release. Most of the published works concentrated on bringing the right candidates into DoD or on retaining them; there was considerably less research attention paid to managing and motivating them. In addition, the studies tended to be about individual employees, with very little about their supervisors and nothing about teams or work groups. How teams are formed, their composition, and how they are managed all have implications for individual career outcomes as well as DoD's ability to support the *National Defense Strategy*. Finally, studies intended to evaluate DoD programs, initiatives, or processes were limited, with the two congressionally mandated

AcqDemo assessments and the evaluation of the Army's Asymmetric Warfare Adaptive Leader Program the notable exceptions. This dearth of evaluation research seems problematic given both the emphasis on evaluation in OPM's knowledge management talent management focus area and multiple studies suggesting DoD's approach to evaluation was inadequate at times.[1] Accordingly, future research focused on evaluation, whether to assess a specific program or initiative or to improve DoD's own evaluation capabilities, would be an especially valuable way to bolster knowledge worker talent management.

---

[1]   U.S. Office of Personnel Management, undated.

Annotated Bibliography of Selected RAND Defense Talent Management Studies, 2013–2020

Asch, Beth J., Michael G. Mattock, and James Hosek, *The Federal Civil Service Workforce: Assessing the Effects on Retention of Pay Freezes, Unpaid Furloughs, and Other Federal-Employee Compensation Changes in the Department of Defense*, Santa Monica, Calif.: RAND Corporation, RR-514-OSD, 2014.

Planners and policymakers must be able to assess how compensation policy, including pay freezes and unpaid furloughs, affects retention. This study begins to extend the dynamic retention model (DRM)—a structural, stochastic, dynamic, discrete-choice model of individual behavior—to federal civil service employment. Models are developed and estimated, using 24 years of data, and then used to simulate the effects of pay freezes and unpaid furloughs. A permanent three-year pay freeze decreases the size of the retained General Service (GS) workforce with at least a baccalaureate degree by 7.3 percent in the steady state. A temporary pay freeze with pay immediately restored has virtually no impact on retention. When pay is restored after ten years, the retained GS workforce falls by 2.8 percent five years after the pay freeze and 3.5 percent ten years after it. An unpaid furlough, similar to the six-day federal furlough in 2013, has no discernible effect on retention. For all subgroups of GS employees for which the model is estimated, the model fit to the actual data is excellent, and all of the model parameter estimates are statistically significant. In future work, the DRM could be extended to provide empirically based simulations of the impact of other policies on retention; to estimate effects on other occupational areas, other pay systems, or specific demographic groups; or to create a "total force" model (military and civilian) of DoD retention dynamics and the effects of compensation on those dynamics.

Ausink, John A., Lisa M. Harrington, Laura Werber, William A. Williams, Jr., John E. Boon, and Michael H. Powell, *Air Force Management of the Defense Acquisition Workforce Development Fund: Opportunities for Improvement,* **Santa Monica, Calif.: RAND Corporation, RR-1486-AF, 2016.**

The Defense Acquisition Workforce Development Fund (DAWDF) was established in 2008 to provide funds for the recruitment, training, and retention of acquisition personnel. Financed by a combination of direct appropriations and funds provided by military departments and defense agencies, the fund is meant to pay for initiatives in three major categories: recruit and hire new acquisition personnel, train and develop members of the existing workforce, and retain and recognize highly skilled personnel. Since the fund's establishment, the U.S. Air Force has contributed more than $600 million to DAWDF and received more than $451 million for various initiatives. The Air Force's Director of Acquisition Career Management (DACM) is responsible for managing the Air Force's share of the money.

In recent years, resources available to the Air Force through the DAWDF have been sufficient to pay for all proposals received by the DACM. Recognizing that this will not always be the case, the DACM asked the RAND Corporation to explore ways to ensure that the funds are used effectively. To do this, we examined legislation, regulations, and other documents related to the fund; interviewed acquisition workforce subject-matter experts and users of DAWDF money in headquarters organizations, major commands (MAJCOM) and centers; analyzed acquisition workforce databases; and interviewed managers in 21 companies that have been recognized by *Fortune* magazine as being among the "100 Best Companies to Work For." We suggest improvements in management processes, describe an evidence-based approach to justify and monitor DAWDF initiatives, and develop an evaluation framework to prioritize DAWDF requests.

Daugherty, Lindsay, Laura Werber, Kristy N. Kamarck, Lisa M. Harrington, and James Gazis, *Officer Accession Planning: A Manual for Estimating Air Force Officer Degree Requirements*, Santa Monica, Calif.: RAND Corporation, TL-196-AF, 2016.

The U.S. Air Force (USAF) sets varying requirements for education to ensure that officer career fields are staffed with individuals that can carry out the required activities to meet mission needs, and many of these educational requirements call for individuals with undergraduate degrees in science, technology, engineering, and mathematics (STEM) fields. RAND research suggests that in some fields, there are substantial gaps between the desired and actual numbers of officers with STEM degrees, and these gaps can lead to issues of reduced capability and a need to pull STEM-degreed officers from other career fields. In addition, it seems that these degree requirements developed through a variety of methods that are not always evidence based, suggesting that a more data-driven approach to developing these requirements is needed. This manual describes the process developed by RAND researchers to estimate STEM degree needs for USAF career fields. Specifically, RAND developed an approach and documented the approach in a draft manual, implemented the draft manual through technical assistance with five career fields in 2013 and 2014, and refined the manual based on the implementation experience. Given the approach was intended to ultimately be used by Career Field Managers (CFMs) and their staff without RAND's involvement, RAND sought to create an approach that provided rigor yet was feasible given the resources available to CFMs.

Gates, Susan M., Brian Phillips, Michael H. Powell, Elizabeth Roth, and Joyce S. Marks, *Analyses of the Department of Defense Acquisition Workforce: Update to Methods and Results Through FY 2017*, Santa Monica, Calif.: RAND Corporation, RR-2492-OSD, 2018.

The defense acquisition workforce is charged with providing the Department of Defense (DoD) with the management, technical, and business capabilities needed to execute defense acquisition programs from start to finish. This workforce must itself be managed so that the right numbers of the right personnel are in the right positions at the right time. Since 2006, RAND has been helping develop data-based tools to support analysis of this workforce. This volume updates RAND's 2008 and 2013 reports by documenting revisions to methods, providing descriptive information on the workforce through fiscal year 2017, analyzing characteristics of recent cohorts entering DoD's civilian acquisition workforce, and describing the evolving policy environment.

Guo, Christopher, Philip Hall-Partyka, and Susan M. Gates, *Retention and Promotion of High-Quality Civil Service Workers in the Department of Defense Acquisition Workforce,* **Santa Monica, Calif.: RAND Corporation, RR-748-OSD, 2014.**

The defense acquisition workforce (AW) includes more than 151,000 military and civilian personnel who provide a range of acquisition, technology, and logistics support (products and services) to the nation's warfighters. This report examines data from Defense Manpower Data Center files and draws from previous related RAND analyses to address questions about factors that affect personnel retention and career advancement in the AW. First, it examines available measures of personnel quality and explores whether personnel retention and career advancement vary by quality. A higher average performance rating is generally associated with an increased hazard of separation (decreased retention). On the other hand, individuals with advanced education degrees (bachelor's, master's, or PhD) are more likely to be retained than those with less than a bachelor's degree. Second, the report describes the characteristics of workers who rise to the senior executive service within the AW. Third, it explores how being in the Acquisition Demonstration pay plan or another demonstration pay plan affects retention, after controlling for workforce quality metrics. People who were in the Acquisition Demonstration pay plan and, in fact, any demonstration pay plan were retained longer than those in the General Schedule.

Hardison, Chaitra M., Leslie Adrienne Payne, John A. Hamm, Angela Clague, Jacqueline Torres, David Schulker, and John S. Crown, *Attracting, Recruiting, and Retaining Successful Cyberspace Operations Officers: Cyber Workforce Interview Findings*, Santa Monica, Calif.: RAND Corporation, RR-2618-AF, 2019.

Cybersecurity is one of the most serious security challenges the United States faces. Information networks are central to the functioning of all major weapons systems and critical to day-to-day operations in the Air Force. Offensive cyber capabilities are also central to the Air Force mission. While many factors ultimately contribute to mission success in these cyberspace domains, one area that directly impacts the Air Force's ability to achieve its cyber mission is its officer workforce, and many are concerned with the current health and future state of that workforce. The Air Force is facing a large shortage of field grade cyberspace operations officers, in the near and long term, raising concerns about retention now and in the future. In addition, the Air Force may face stiff competition from the private sector in attracting and retaining top cyber talent. Finally, because many receive highly technical training from the Air Force that further increases their marketability, the Air Force is concerned it may lose talented personnel to the private sector.

To gain insights into key drivers for attracting and retaining cyberspace operations officers and essential characteristics of high-performing personnel, the authors review what is already known about retention issues facing the career field, summarize research on the domestic and military cyber workforces, and conduct interviews with a wide cross-section of individuals in the Air Force and the private sector. The authors ascertain sources of satisfaction and dissatisfaction that might affect retention and recruiting and make recommendations for how to address them.

Hardison, Chaitra M., Mikhail Zaydman, Tobi A. Oluwatola, Anna Rosefsky Saavedra, Thomas Bush, Heather Peterson, and Susan G. Straus, *360-Degree Assessments: Are They the Right Tool for the U.S. Military?*, **Santa Monica, Calif.: RAND Corporation, RR-998-OSD, 2015.**

In response to the National Defense Authorization Act for fiscal year 2014, which directed the Secretary of Defense to assess "the feasibility of including a 360-degree assessment [360] approach . . . as part of performance evaluation reports," the Office of the Under Secretary of Defense for Personnel and Readiness (OUSD/P&R) asked the RAND Corporation to provide an outside assessment of the advisability of using 360s for evaluation purposes in the military. In addition, OUSD/P&R also requested information on the role of 360s more broadly. Thus, this report explores the pros and cons of using 360s for evaluation and development purposes in the military. The research was based on information gleaned from a number of sources: existing research literature and expert guidance on 360 best practices; policy documents and other sources summarizing current performance and promotion practices in the military services, including the use of 360s; and interviews with a sample of stakeholders and subject-matter experts in the Department of Defense. The results suggest that using 360 feedback as part of the military performance evaluation system is not advisable at this time, though the services could benefit from using 360s as a tool for leader development and to gain an aggregate view of leadership across the force.

Harrington, Lisa M., Lindsay Daugherty, S. Craig Moore, and Tara L. Terry, *Air Force–Wide Needs for Science, Technology, Engineering, and Mathematics (STEM) Academic Degrees,* **Santa Monica, Calif.: RAND Corporation, RR-659-AF, 2014.**

In evaluating the health of its science, technology, engineering, and mathematics workforce, the U.S. Air Force has focused on functional areas where STEM degrees are mandatory. To date, there has been no rigorous review of the needs for STEM academic degrees in other functional areas. Understating the needs for officers and civilians with

STEM degrees can diminish the Air Force's ability to maintain the technical skills it heavily relies upon to support air, space, and cyberspace operations. Analysis must begin with a definition of STEM versus non-STEM degrees. RAND researchers established a set of broad academic disciplinary groups that should be considered in the set of STEM degrees, as well as disciplines at the most detailed levels of Air Force degree codes. This categorization has been approved as the Air Force definition of STEM.

Career field managers across the Air Force were interviewed and asked to identify the STEM academic degrees necessary now and in the future for particular missions in their functional areas. Senior functional authorities at the two- and three-star level reviewed and, in some cases, revised what their own career field managers identified as STEM needs and validated the overall direction and the numbers of these degree requirements. Although this approach lacks a method to determine the magnitude of future STEM needs in the programs identified, it does point to specific areas that the Air Force should review for emerging STEM needs, especially in light of force management actions in key technology areas.

Knopp, Bradley M., Sina Beaghley, Aaron Frank, Rebeca Orrie, and Michael Watson, *Defining the Roles, Responsibilities, and Functions for Data Science Within the Defense Intelligence Agency*, Santa Monica, Calif.: RAND Corporation, RR-1582-DIA, 2016.

This report addresses and recommends potential methods for the Defense Intelligence Agency (DIA) to identify, hire, and organize data scientists. The authors examine data science activities in the private sector and university-level data science training and also explore hiring and retention options for creating a data science capability within DIA. They also examine the results of interviews with DIA employees. The authors recommend that DIA create its own data science capability with a mix of government experts and contractors capable of managing activities unique to military intelligence operations and that DIA establish a center of excellence to oversee and promote data science activities, development, and training.

Lewis, Jennifer Lamping, Laura Werber, Cameron Wright, Irina Danescu, Jessica Hwang, and Lindsay Daugherty, *2016 Assessment of the Civilian Acquisition Workforce Personnel Demonstration Project*, Santa Monica, Calif.: RAND Corporation, RR-1783-OSD, 2017.

In August 2015, René Thomas-Rizzo, director, Human Capital Initiatives, Office of the Under Secretary of Defense for Acquisition, Technology, and Logistics, asked the RAND Corporation to undertake a study to accomplish the fiscal year (FY) 2016 assessment of the Civilian Acquisition Workforce Personnel Demonstration Project (AcqDemo) mandated in the National Defense Authorization Act (NDAA) of FY 2011. AcqDemo aims to provide a system that retains, recognizes, and rewards employees for their contributions and supports their personal and professional development. The assessment used multiple data sources to evaluate how well AcqDemo has performed with respect to these goals. The assessment directly addresses the original 12 criteria enumerated in the NDAA, as well as five new criteria specified by the AcqDemo Program Office. These criteria call for a look at the following: AcqDemo's key features pertaining to hiring, appointments, and performance appraisal; the adequacy of its guidance, protections for diversity, efforts to ensure fairness and transparency, and means used to involve employees in improving AcqDemo; AcqDemo's impact on career outcomes, such as compensation, promotion, and retention, particularly with respect to similar outcomes for the General Schedule workforce; AcqDemo's ability to support the acquisition mission. The RAND team found that some aspects of AcqDemo are performing well, while others leave room for improvement.

Li, Jennifer J., and Lindsay Daugherty, *Training Cyber Warriors: What Can Be Learned from Defense Language Training?*, Santa Monica, Calif.: RAND Corporation, RR-476-OSD, 2015.

As the importance of cyber operations in national security grows, the U.S. military's ability to ensure a robust cyber workforce becomes increasingly important in protecting the nation. A particular concern has been the growing need for cyber warriors: highly trained and specialized individuals who engage in offensive and defensive operations. The authors seek to help those planning future training for cyber warriors by highlighting what can be learned from another specialty: defense language. While there is no perfect analogy between cyber personnel and another segment of the national security workforce, a number of similarities exist between the need for language skills and cyber warrior expertise, including the need for a highly specialized skill that requires extensive training, the critical role of the skill in mission effectiveness, a need to quickly build capacity, and a potentially limited pipeline of qualified candidates. In this exploratory study, the authors examine what the military services and national security agencies have done to train linguists—personnel with skills in critical languages other than English—and the kinds of language training provided to build and maintain this segment of the workforce. They draw from published documents, research literature, and interviews of experts in both language and cyber. Among key findings, the authors find that shared definitions and metrics are an important first step, training must be closely aligned with mission needs, efforts should focus on building a strong pipeline of candidates, and training must be aligned with overall workforce management efforts.

Libicki, Martin C., David Senty, and Julia Pollak, *Hackers Wanted: An Examination of the Cybersecurity Labor Market*, Santa Monica, Calif.: RAND Corporation, RR-430, 2014.

There is a general perception that there is a shortage of cybersecurity professionals within the United States, and a particular shortage of these professionals within the federal government, working on national security as well as intelligence. Shortages of this nature complicate securing the nation's networks and may leave the United States ill prepared to carry out conflict in cyberspace.

RAND examined the current status of the labor market for cybersecurity professionals—with an emphasis on their being employed to defend the United States. This effort was in three parts: first, a review of the literature; second, interviews with managers and educators of cybersecurity professionals, supplemented by reportage; and third, an examination of the economic literature about labor markets. RAND also disaggregated the broad definition of "cybersecurity professionals" to unearth skills differentiation as relevant to this study.

In general, we support the use of market forces (and preexisting government programs) to address the strong demand for cybersecurity professionals in the longer run. Increases in educational opportunities and compensation packages will draw more workers into the profession over time. Cybersecurity professionals take time to reach their potential; drastic steps taken today to increase their quantity and quality would not bear fruit for another five to ten years. By then, the current concern over cybersecurity could easily abate, driven by new technology and more secure architectures. Pushing too many people into the profession now could leave an overabundance of highly trained and narrowly skilled individuals who could better be serving national needs in other vocations.

Lim, Nelson, Abigail Haddad, Dwayne M. Butler, and Katheryn Giglio, *First Steps Toward Improving DoD STEM Workforce Diversity: Response to the 2012 Department of Defense STEM Diversity Summit*, Santa Monica, Calif.: RAND Corporation, RR-329-OSD, 2013.

In FY 2011–2012, leaders from the Executive Branch and the Department of Defense (DoD) offered directives and guidance intended to increase diversity across all federal agencies. In response, the DoD Research and Engineering Enterprise and DoD's Office of Diversity Management and Equal Opportunity held a two-day summit in November 2012 on improving diversity within the science, technology, engineering, and mathematics (STEM) workforce. This report supports the efforts of the DoD STEM Diversity Summit by providing suggestions for future research, analysis, and action. The authors describe policies that discuss the federal government's values and priorities regarding diversity in the federal workforce; offer a closer look at current STEM demographics, including those of the DoD's STEM workforce; discuss current STEM-diversity outreach programs, highlighting the types of data that should be collected in the future; and offer recommendations for DoD leaders to consider as they move forward with their efforts to diversify the STEM workforce.

Lim, Nelson, Abigail Haddad, and Lindsay Daugherty, *Implementation of the DoD Diversity and Inclusion Strategic Plan: A Framework for Change Through Accountability,* **Santa Monica, Calif.: RAND Corporation, RR-333-OSD, 2013.**

Two recent policy documents lay out a new vision for diversity in the U.S. Department of Defense (DoD): the Military Leadership Diversity Commission's *From Representation to Inclusion: Diversity Leadership for the 21st-Century Military* and the *Department of Defense Diversity and Inclusion Strategic Plan, 2012–2017.* These documents define the mission, set goals for diversity, and provide a general strategic framework for achieving these goals. The purpose of this report is to provide a framework to support DoD in the implementation of its strategic plan and to ensure that the resources devoted to these efforts are targeted for long-term success. The framework emphasizes the creation of an enduring accountability system; categorizes the strategic initiatives specified in DoD's strategic plan along three key dimensions—compliance, communication, and coordination ("the three *Cs*"); and prioritizes them across time—short, medium, and long term. The framework can help all DoD components work toward the vision described in the strategic plan in a deliberate, synchronized effort by complying with current laws, regulations, and directives; communicating effectively to internal as well as external stakeholders; and coordinating efforts to ensure continuing change.

Lytell, Maria C., Kirsten M. Keller, Beth Katz, Jefferson P. Marquis, and Jerry M. Sollinger, *Diversity Leadership in the U.S. Department of Defense: Analysis of the Key Roles, Responsibilities, and Attributes of Diversity Leaders,* **Santa Monica, Calif.: RAND Corporation, RR-1148-OSD, 2016.**

This study identifies the knowledge, skills, abilities, and other characteristics (KSAOs) needed in individuals who will be responsible for implementing strategic diversity plans in the U.S. Department of Defense (DoD). The authors interviewed more than 60 diversity leaders in industry, the public sector (including DoD), and academia and reviewed relevant scientific literature, education programs, and advertised job requirements. The study found that primary roles and responsibilities for diversity leaders include strategic leadership, stakeholder engagement, tracking diversity trends, and human resources–related activities. To carry out these responsibilities, diversity leaders would ideally have the following KSAOs: interpersonal skills; business expertise; leadership skills; equal employment opportunity, affirmative action, and diversity knowledge and skills; a driven personality and commitment to diversity; analytical abilities and skills; critical thinking and problem-solving skills; and multicultural competence. Certain KSAOs are harder to develop than others (e.g., personality attributes and motivation) and should form the basis of selection of diversity leaders. Other KSAOs, such as problem-solving, communication, and technical skills, are easier to develop and may be enhanced through training and education. The study recommends a three-step plan for DoD to help determine how to train and educate future DoD diversity leaders: (1) determine whether there should be a separate professional development track for diversity and inclusion personnel, (2) determine training and education requirements by focusing on those KSAOs more amenable to development, and (3) determine the best means for fulfilling those requirements (e.g., whether to outsource the training).

Lytell, Maria C., Susan G. Straus, Chad C. Serena, Geoffrey E. Grimm, James L. Doty III, Jennie W. Wenger, Andrea M. Abler, Andrew M. Naber, Clifford A. Grammich, and Eric S. Fowler, *Assessing Competencies and Proficiency of Army Intelligence Analysts Across the Career Life Cycle,* **Santa Monica, Calif.: RAND Corporation, RR-1851-A, 2017.**

Army military intelligence (MI) analysts work in increasingly complex and dynamic operational environments requiring intangible competencies, such as critical thinking (CT) and adaptability. This report describes the development and implementation of a process to assess key analytic competencies and proficiency of the Army's analysts in the 35F military occupational specialty and the design of a protocol for ongoing evaluation. The study included subject-matter expert interviews and document review to identify key analytic tasks for 35F analysts; a review of research regarding competencies associated with intelligence analysis and measures of those competencies; and a field study assessing competencies, life-cycle factors, training proficiency among junior analysts, and job proficiency among junior and midgrade analysts. Analysis of training proficiency results shows that analysts with greater general mental ability had higher grade-point averages and better odds of graduating from initial skill training than other analysts had. Results comparing junior and midgrade analysts indicate that both groups have few opportunities to perform MI tasks on the job. Both groups were similar in most competencies, but midgrade analysts demonstrated higher CT skills than junior analysts did. Differences between junior and midgrade analysts in job proficiency were mixed; junior analysts performed better on some criteria and midgrade analysts performed better on others. However, job proficiency scores were relatively low across groups, and few competencies predicted job proficiency; these findings could be a result of skill decay or low motivation of study participants.

Markel, M. Wade, Jefferson P. Marquis, Peter Schirmer, Sean Robson, Lisa Saum-Manning, Katherine C. Hastings, Katharina Ley Best, Christina Panis, Alyssa Ramos, and Barbara Bicksler, *Career Development for the Department of Defense Security Cooperation Workforce,* **Santa Monica, Calif.: RAND Corporation, RR-1846-OSD, 2018.**

Security cooperation's importance, scale, and complexity have grown substantially in recent years, but efforts to develop and manage the Department of Defense security cooperation workforce have lagged. This study informs the development of career models for the security cooperation workforce, assesses potential requirements for competencies and experience, and identifies potential job families within the workforce to facilitate management.

Matthews, Miriam, Bruce R. Orvis, David Schulker, Kimberly Curry Hall, Abigail Haddad, Stefan Zavislan, and Nelson Lim, *Hispanic Representation in the Department of Defense Civilian Workforce: Trend and Barrier Analysis,* **Santa Monica, Calif.: RAND Corporation, RR-1699-OSD, 2017.**

Hispanics are less represented in the federal government workforce than in the U.S. civilian labor force, and they are particularly underrepresented in the U.S. Department of Defense (DoD) civilian workforce. Although previous analyses have demonstrated that Hispanics are underrepresented in DoD, research has not yet considered employment barriers for Hispanics across DoD agencies. In this report, the authors provide information that might help DoD address Hispanic underrepresentation in its civilian workforce. They examine trends in Hispanic employment in the DoD, non-DoD federal, and civilian workforces. They also explore whether DoD labor-force characteristics might account for Hispanic underrepresentation in DoD. In addition, the authors examine observed trends in job applicants and applications to DoD. They also present findings from interviews that they conducted with DoD hiring managers and supervisors and representatives of Hispanic-serving institutions. They conclude with recommendations for DoD to consider as part of its efforts to address Hispanic underrepresentation in the DoD civilian workforce.

Matthews, Miriam, David Schulker, Kimberly Curry Hall, Abigail Haddad, and Nelson Lim, *Representation of Persons with Targeted Disabilities: An Analysis of Barriers to Employment in the Department of Defense Civilian Workforce,* **Santa Monica, Calif.: RAND Corporation, RR-2297-OSD, 2018.**

Although a representative federal workforce is a strategic personnel priority in the U.S. Department of Defense (DoD), certain demographic groups have historically been underrepresented and may continue to face employment barriers. One such group includes people with targeted disabilities (PWTD), who are the focus of this report. The federal workforce has a 2-percent representation goal for the employment of persons with specific disabilities or health conditions. Previous assessments have shown that DoD has not met the federal employment goal for PWTD.

To address this issue, RAND researchers sought to identify and address current employment barriers within DoD that PWTD may experience and recommend actions DoD can take to increase employment of PWTD in its civilian workforce. To do so, they analyzed personnel records and data on applicants and applications. They also interviewed representatives from colleges and universities, DoD and its components, and other federal agencies. Finally, they surveyed DoD hiring managers and supervisors on topics addressing the employment of PWTD.

The analyses demonstrated that DoD did not meet the 2-percent representation goal during the years for which we have data (2008–2013). In addition, DoD had a lower representation of PWTD than the non-DoD federal workforce, and this difference in PWTD representation was not explained by workforce characteristics. Interviewees indicated that students lack awareness of DoD civilian job opportunities. Survey results suggested that DoD employees tend to hold positive perceptions of PWTD. However, limited knowledge regarding disability employment goals, programs, and resources might be an employment barrier for PWTD.

Nataraj, Shanthi, Christopher Guo, Philip Hall-Partyka, Susan M. Gates, and Douglas Yeung, *Options for Department of Defense Total Workforce Supply and Demand Analysis: Potential Approaches and Available Data Sources,* **Santa Monica, Calif.: RAND Corporation, RR-543-OSD, 2014.**

This report provides a review of approaches used in the private sector and in government organizations for determining workforce supply and demand and describes the data sources available to U.S. Department of Defense managers to support workforce analysis from a total force perspective. Each of the approaches discussed in this document has strengths and weaknesses. The best approach will depend on the question that needs to be addressed and the resources (data and expertise) available. The report highlights critical workforce analysis choices facing managers regarding the scope of analysis, the level of aggregation, the type of projection techniques that will be used, the time period over which historical analysis of projections will be conducted, and the data sources to be used. The authors describe existing data sources and discuss their strengths and weaknesses as an input into the workforce supply and demand analysis approaches described in this report. They also evaluate existing data sources in light of their ability to support workforce gap analyses at the organizational and occupational levels, as well as by competency.

Paul, Christopher, Isaac R. Porche III, and Elliot Axelband, *The Other Quiet Professionals: Lessons for Future Cyber Forces from the Evolution of Special Forces,* **Santa Monica, Calif.: RAND Corporation, RR-780-A, 2014.**

With the establishment of U.S. Cyber Command in 2010, the cyber force is gaining visibility and authority, but challenges remain, particularly in the areas of acquisition and personnel recruitment and career progression. A review of commonalities, similarities, and differences between the still-nascent U.S. cyber force and early U.S. special operations forces, conducted in 2010, offers salient lessons for the future direction of U.S. cyber forces. Although U.S. special operations forces (SOF) have a long and storied history and now represent a mature, long-standing capability, they struggled in the 1970s and 1980s before winning an institutional champion and joint home in the form of U.S. Special Operations Command. U.S. cyber forces similarly represent a new but critical set of military capabilities. Both SOF and cyber forces are, at their operating core, small teams of highly skilled specialists, and both communities value skilled personnel above all else. Irregular warfare and SOF doctrine lagged operational activities, and the same is true of the cyber force. Early SOF, like the contemporary cyber force, lacked organizational cohesion, a unified development strategy, and institutionalized training. Perhaps most importantly, the capabilities of both forces have traditionally been inadequate to meet demand. The analogy holds for issues of acquisition, the two forces' relationship with the conventional military, their applicability across the spectrum of combat, and their historic need for a strong advocate for reform. The analogy is not perfect, however. In terms of core capabilities, force accession, and tradition, the forces are also very different. But even these differences offer fundamental lessons for both the U.S. Department of Defense and the U.S. Army with regard to the future and potential of the cyber force.

Porche, Isaac R., Caolionn O'Connell, John S. Davis II, Bradley Wilson, Chad C. Serena, Tracy C. McCausland, Erin-Elizabeth Johnson, Brian D. Wisniewski, and Michael Vasseur, *Cyber Power Potential of the Army's Reserve Component,* **Santa Monica, Calif.: RAND Corporation, RR-1490-A, 2017.**

The military services are formalizing and bolstering their contribution to the nation's cyber force, known as the U.S. Cyber Command Cyber Mission Force. As a part of a Total Force approach, the Army is considering using both active component and reserve component (RC) personnel to fill the Cyber Mission Force and other requirements in support of Army units.

This report identifies the number of Army RC personnel with cyber skills, to help identify ways in which these soldiers can be leveraged to conduct Army cyber operations. This report also describes the broader challenges and opportunities that the use of RC personnel presents.

To study this issue, the authors first performed a thorough review of past studies, government reports, and relevant literature. Next, they analyzed data from the Civilian Employment Information database and the Work Experience File database, and they performed analyses of social media data from LinkedIn profiles, which include self-reported cyber skills among reservists. They reviewed and assessed the knowledge, skills, and abilities (KSAs) defined for Cyber Mission Force roles in order to determine the percentage of these KSAs that can be acquired in the private sector. Finally, they conducted a survey of more than 1,200 guardsmen and reservists.

Based on both quantitative and qualitative analyses, the authors find that relevant information technology and cyber skills are in abundance in the private sector. As a result, there are tens of thousands of "citizen-soldiers"—that is, soldiers in the Army RC—that have the potential to support the Army's cyber mission needs and/or the propensity to learn cyber skills.

Robson, Sean, Bonnie L. Triezenberg, Samantha E. DiNicola, Lindsey Polley, John S. Davis II, and Maria C. Lytell, *Software Acquisition Workforce Initiative for the Department of Defense: Initial Competency Development and Preparation for Validation,* **Santa Monica, Calif.: RAND Corporation, RR-3145-OSD, 2020.**

The U.S. Department of Defense (DoD) seeks to advance the ability of its software acquisition workforce to rapidly and reliably deliver complex software-dependent capabilities through an enhanced understanding of technical competencies, improvements to education and training, and guidance for workforce management and assessment. Focusing on three primary acquisition career fields—information technology, engineering, and program management—the authors review existing competency models used by DoD and commercial industry, along with industry trends and modern software practices, and gather feedback from stakeholders and subject-matter experts to develop a model consisting of 48 competencies organized by topic: problem identification, solution identification, development planning, transition and sustainment planning, system architecture design, software construction management, software program management, mission assurance, and professional competencies. They also review existing courses offered by the Defense Acquisition University, other DoD institutions, and private and public universities to determine whether and to what extent the courses offer software training and education that corresponds with these competencies, and to identify ways to address potential gaps. Although there is no currently accepted government job title or occupational series for software professionals, and although the competency model thus affords limited utility for assessing current workforce capability, the authors present options for tracking and managing the software acquisition workforce, as well as further steps toward validating the competency model.

Ross, Shirley M., Rebecca Herman, Irina A. Chindea, Samantha E. Dinicola, and Amy Grace Donohue, *Optimizing the Contributions of Air Force Civilian STEM Workforce,* **Santa Monica, Calif.: RAND Corporation, RR-4234-AF, 2020.**

The U.S. Air Force's ability to accomplish national security goals relies heavily on research advances in the science, technology, engineering, and mathematics (STEM) fields. The current shortage of STEM professionals has a direct impact on how the Air Force carries out its mission. Addressing the gap in the Air Force's civilian STEM workforce and optimizing the productivity of its existing civilian STEM employees falls squarely within the Air Force's responsibility. Because of concerns over the shortage of civilian STEM professionals, especially those with advanced degrees, Air Force leadership asked RAND Project AIR FORCE (PAF) to explore the existing academic and professional literature on STEM workforce to gain insights into how organizations such as the Air Force should manage, support, and organize their current civilian STEM workers to best leverage their talents and thereby maximize performance.

PAF engaged in an extensive survey of the relevant literature to answer this question. First, the authors provided a brief overview of the differences between modern knowledge organizations, in contrast to traditional manufacturing or industrial organizations. Second, they described the characteristics of work that most appeal to STEM workers and drive their productivity. Third, the authors discussed human-capital functions that relate to the performance of STEM workers. Fourth, they discussed the changes in organizational structure most likely to foster STEM employees' productivity and innovation. Finally, the last section of this report summarizes the researchers' findings and recommendations.

Schmidt, Lara, Caolionn O'Connell, Hirokazu Miyake, Akhil R. Shah, Joshua William Baron, Geof Nieboer, Rose Jourdan, David Senty, Zev Winkelman, Louise Taggart, Susanne Sondergaard, and Neil Robinson, *Cyber Practices: What Can the U.S. Air Force Learn from the Commercial Sector?,* **Santa Monica, Calif.: RAND Corporation, RR-847-AF, 2015.**

To meet the challenges of the cyberspace era—including the rapid rate of change in technology, the growing cyber threat, and the need to integrate cyber with operations in other warfighting domains—the U.S. Air Force (USAF) must find effective ways to organize, train, and equip its cyber forces. This report identifies approaches to cyber organizational and workforce issues. Specifically, it describes efforts to identify successful processes and practices from the commercial sector that might be applicable to USAF. To ascertain successful commercial practices, the authors took a twofold approach: a wide-ranging literature review and interviews with a carefully crafted set of commercial organizations, selected for their similarities to USAF and for their reputations of cyber excellence. Companies were identified to be similar to USAF in size, cyber functions performed, exposure to cyber threats, and operational environment. The authors found strong parallels in the commercial sector for Department of Defense information network operations and defensive cyber operations. Although none of the companies interviewed were as large as USAF or required to function in deployed and contested operating environments, the commercial practices described in the report are likely to be applicable to USAF and result in effectiveness and efficiency gains. The authors describe the basis for each practice, the benefits it conveys, and how it could be implemented by USAF.

Schulker, David, and Miriam Matthews, *Women's Representation in the U.S. Department of Defense Workforce: Addressing the Influence of Veterans' Employment,* **Santa Monica, Calif.: RAND Corporation, RR-2458-OSD, 2018.**

To indicate where barriers to equal employment opportunity might be amenable to personnel policy changes, U.S. Equal Employment Opportunity Commission regulations direct federal agencies and departments to compare their workforce demographics with those of the civilian labor force (CLF). Persistent discrepancies between employees who work for the U.S. Department of Defense (DoD) and those in the CLF prompted a formal analysis of these workforce differences and potential barriers. This report represents an exploratory effort examining the relatively low level of women's representation and testing the utility of alternative methods in better understanding workforce dynamics.

Many long-standing policies explicitly favor employing veterans in the federal government. The fact that most veterans are men creates the possibility of a trade-off between goals for employing veterans and Equal Employment Opportunity Commission workforce demographic goals. The researchers for this study assessed both static and long-run representation with changes in hiring practices, as well as with varying retention levels.

Straus, Susan G., Tracy C. Krueger, Geoffrey E. Grimm, and Katheryn Giglio, *Malleability and Measurement of Army Leader Attributes: Personnel Development in the U.S. Army*, Santa Monica, Calif.: RAND Corporation, RR-1583-A, 2018.

Army leaders face a myriad of challenges that demand a wide range of knowledge, skills, abilities, and other characteristics. Army Doctrine Reference Publication 6-22, *Army Leadership*, delineates the attributes and competencies that leaders should possess in the Army Leader Requirements Model (ALRM). This study supports the Army's leadership development and training efforts by examining psychological constructs associated with intellect, presence, and character attributes specified in the ALRM.

One objective of this report is to review research evidence for the extent to which key constructs can be developed through training and education. Findings indicate that some constructs, such as physical fitness, creative thinking skills, and resilience, are amenable to change through training and education, whereas others, such as general mental ability, are more stable. Other constructs, such as generalized self-efficacy and expertise, may be amenable to change, but development requires substantial time and effort.

A second objective of the report is to identify established measures of constructs associated with ALRM attributes. For most constructs, there are numerous measures available, consisting largely of tests and surveys. Conclusions in the report address considerations for selection of measures, designs for studying training and education interventions, and recommendations for routine data collection for use in job placement and ongoing study efforts. Findings from this review are relevant not only to leadership and to the Army but to the development and assessment of personnel in a wide range of positions and organizations.

Straus, Susan G., Michael G. Shanley, Carra S. Sims, Bryan W. Hallmark, Anna Rosefsky Saavedra, Stoney Trent, and Sean Duggan, *Innovative Leader Development: Evaluation of the U.S. Army Asymmetric Warfare Adaptive Leader Program,* **Santa Monica, Calif.: RAND Corporation, RR-504-A, 2014.**

The Asymmetric Warfare Group offers the Asymmetric Warfare Adaptive Leader Program (AWALP)—a 10-day course designed to enhance adaptive performance in leaders and promote innovative solutions in training in support of unified land operations. This report describes results of a systematic evaluation of AWALP, offers recommendations to improve the course, and provides recommendations for ongoing evaluation of AWALP and other courses or events that address adaptive performance and acquisition of other intangible skills. The study used a pretest-posttest design and collected data from 104 students who participated in AWALP. Results show substantial improvement in training outcomes, including students' self-efficacy for being adaptive and leading adaptive teams and knowledge of course concepts. Graduates also reported that they were applying course concepts on the job after returning to their units. In addition, students had exceptionally favorable reactions to AWALP and remained extremely positive about the course three months after graduation. Results indicate few needs for improvement in the course; the most important area to address is challenges in applying concepts on the job because of the command climate and entrenched leadership. Recommendations for ongoing evaluation focus on obtaining additional measures of adaptive performance, particularly to establish the impact of AWALP on subsequent job performance. The current success of AWALP suggests that its approach to training might be usefully expanded in the Army, and we discuss strategies to achieve broader dissemination. Finally, we describe how the methods used in this study might be applied to evaluating related training in other contexts.

Wenger, Jennie W., Caolionn O'Connell, and Maria C. Lytell, *Retaining the Army's Cyber Expertise*, Santa Monica, Calif.: RAND Corporation, RR-1978-A, 2017.

In 2014, the Army established the cyber career field as a basic branch, which includes the 17C military occupational specialty for enlisted cyber operations specialists. These soldiers require extensive training, and Army leadership is concerned that they will be lured away by lucrative jobs in the civilian labor market. This report describes findings that will help inform the Army's strategy for retaining these 17C soldiers. Our findings indicate that soldiers who qualify for 17C are more likely than others to remain in the Army through their first term; however, they also appear to be somewhat less likely to reenlist. In the civilian sector, information security analysts perform similar duties to 17Cs in the Army, and many information security analysts are veterans. Given that, 17C soldiers who do not reenlist may pursue civilian careers as information security analysts. Although information security analysts have higher wages than many other workers in the American workforce, projected earnings for information security analysts with characteristics similar to those of enlisted soldiers are comparable with military pay. However, the data indicate that the median pay for information security analysts with a college degree is considerably higher than Army enlisted compensation. It is important to note that our analysis focused on the actual wages of information security personnel, not the perceived wages. Retention efforts may be seriously hampered by the perceptions young enlisted soldiers might have regarding their civilian opportunities outside the Army. Therefore, managing this new occupation will require attention.

Werber, Laura, John A. Ausink, Lindsay Daugherty, Brian Phillips, Felix Knutson, and Ryan Haberman, *An Assessment of Gaps in Business Acumen and Knowledge of Industry Within the Defense Acquisition Workforce: A Report Prepared for the U.S. Department of Defense in Compliance with Section 843(c) of the Fiscal Year 2018 National Defense Authorization Act*, Santa Monica, Calif.: RAND Corporation, RR-2825-OSD, 2019.

The U.S. Department of Defense's (DoD's) acquisition workforce (AWF) includes more than 169,000 personnel who are responsible for identifying, developing, buying, and managing goods and services to support the military. In 2018, Congress directed the Under Secretary of Defense for Acquisition and Sustainment to conduct an assessment of gaps in business acumen, knowledge of industry operations, and knowledge of industry motivation present within the AWF and to determine the effectiveness of training and development (T&D) resources offered by providers outside DoD that were available to AWF personnel. RAND was chosen to perform the assessment, and researchers used a mixed-methods approach to do so, including interviews with DoD and industry professionals and reviews of AWF competency models, Defense Acquisition University course offerings, DoD policy, and academic and business literature. The authors found that the lack of standardized definitions obscures the need for knowledge related to business acumen, industry operations, and industry motivation, and while knowledge gaps appear to exist in these areas, the lack of requirements and desired proficiencies further hinders an estimation of the gaps' extent. DoD uses a wide array of internal and external T&D assets to develop the AWF, but training gaps related to these types of knowledge were difficult to determine in part because evidence about the effectiveness of different types of T&D is limited. The authors provide recommendations to DoD to improve how these types of knowledge are assessed and conferred as well as recommendations to Congress for incentivizing DoD's use of external T&D providers.

Werber, Laura, Paul W. Mayberry, Mark Doboga, and Diana Gehlhaus Carew, *Support for DoD Supervisors in Addressing Poor Employee Performance: A Holistic Approach,* **Santa Monica, Calif.: RAND Corporation, RR-2665-OSD, 2018.**

In 2017, the Office of Management and Budget (OMB) issued a memorandum that instructed federal agencies to develop actionable, measurable plans to maximize employee performance, including rewards for high performers and penalties for poor performers. At the time of the memorandum's release, the U.S. Department of Defense (DoD) already had changes under way intended to maximize the performance of its civilian workforce, the largest civilian workforce in the federal government at approximately 732,000 appropriated employees and also one of the most diverse in terms of occupations.

Recent evidence—specifically, the facts that 25 percent of DoD supervisors reported directly supervising at least one poor performer and that roughly 60 percent of these supervisors agreed that a poor performer would negatively affect the ability of other subordinates to do their own jobs—coupled with OMB's 2017 memorandum, motivated this study. In this report, the authors use interviews with human resources practitioners, survey responses from DoD supervisors, and past research to (1) identify promising policies, procedures, and structures for maximizing employee performance, with emphasis on assisting supervisors of poor-performing personnel; and (2) develop recommendations on how best to support supervisors responsible for managing the poor-performing DoD employees. The framework they present calls for developing, supporting, and professionalizing supervisors in conjunction with assessing and reporting key performance-related outcomes.

References

Asch, Beth J., Michael G. Mattock, and James Hosek, *The Federal Civil Service Workforce: Assessing the Effects on Retention of Pay Freezes, Unpaid Furloughs, and Other Federal-Employee Compensation Changes in the Department of Defense*, Santa Monica, Calif.: RAND Corporation, RR-514-OSD, 2014. As of February 23, 2021: https://www.rand.org/pubs/research_reports/RR514.html

Ausink, John A., Lisa M. Harrington, Laura Werber, William A. Williams, Jr., John E. Boon, and Michael H. Powell, *Air Force Management of the Defense Acquisition Workforce Development Fund: Opportunities for Improvement*, Santa Monica, Calif.: RAND Corporation, RR-1486-AF, 2016. As of February 23, 2021: https://www.rand.org/pubs/research_reports/RR1486.html

Daugherty, Lindsay, Laura Werber, Kristy N. Kamarck, Lisa M. Harrington, and James Gazis, *Officer Accession Planning: A Manual for Estimating Air Force Officer Degree Requirements*, Santa Monica, Calif.: RAND Corporation, TL-196-AF, 2016. As of February 23, 2021:
https://www.rand.org/pubs/tools/TL196.html

Drucker, Peter F. "The Age of Social Transformation," *The Atlantic Monthly*, Vol. 274, No. 5, 1994, pp. 53–80.

Gates, Susan M., Brian Phillips, Michael H. Powell, Elizabeth Roth, and Joyce S. Marks, *Analyses of the Department of Defense Acquisition Workforce: Update to Methods and Results Through FY 2017*, Santa Monica, Calif.: RAND Corporation, RR-2492-OSD, 2018. As of February 23, 2021:
https://www.rand.org/pubs/research_reports/RR2492.html

Gere, Pete, "Secretary of the Army Statement on the Army's Strategic Imperatives," Testimony Before the Senate Armed Services Committee, United States Senate, First Session, 110th Congress, Washington D.C., November 15, 2007.

Guo, Christopher, Philip Hall-Partyka, and Susan M. Gates, *Retention and Promotion of High-Quality Civil Service Workers in the Department of Defense Acquisition Workforce*, Santa Monica, Calif.: RAND Corporation, RR-748-OSD, 2014. As of February 23, 2021:
https://www.rand.org/pubs/research_reports/RR748.html

Hardison, Chaitra M., Leslie Adrienne Payne, John A. Hamm, Angela Clague, Jacqueline Torres, David Schulker, and John S. Crown, *Attracting, Recruiting, and Retaining Successful Cyberspace Operations Officers: Cyber Workforce Interview Findings*, Santa Monica, Calif.: RAND Corporation, RR-2618-AF, 2019. As of February 23, 2021:
https://www.rand.org/pubs/research_reports/RR2618.html

Hardison, Chaitra M., Mikhail Zaydman, Tobi A. Oluwatola, Anna Rosefsky Saavedra, Thomas Bush, Heather Peterson, and Susan G. Straus, *360-Degree Assessments: Are They the Right Tool for the U.S. Military?*, Santa Monica, Calif.: RAND Corporation, RR-998-OSD, 2015. As of February 23, 2021:
https://www.rand.org/pubs/research_reports/RR998.html

Harrington, Lisa M., Lindsay Daugherty, S. Craig Moore, and Tara L. Terry, *Air Force–Wide Needs for Science, Technology, Engineering, and Mathematics (STEM) Academic Degrees*, Santa Monica, Calif.: RAND Corporation, RR-659-AF, 2014. As of February 23, 2021:
https://www.rand.org/pubs/research_reports/RR659.html

Knopp, Bradley M., Sina Beaghley, Aaron Frank, Rebeca Orrie, and Michael Watson, *Defining the Roles, Responsibilities, and Functions for Data Science Within the Defense Intelligence Agency*, Santa Monica, Calif.: RAND Corporation, RR-1582-DIA, 2016. As of February 23, 2021:
https://www.rand.org/pubs/research_reports/RR1582.html

Lewis, Jennifer Lamping, Laura Werber, Cameron Wright, Irina Danescu, Jessica Hwang, and Lindsay Daugherty, *2016 Assessment of the Civilian Acquisition Workforce Personnel Demonstration Project*, Santa Monica, Calif.: RAND Corporation, RR-1783-OSD, 2017. As of February 23, 2021:
https://www.rand.org/pubs/research_reports/RR1783.html

Li, Jennifer J., and Lindsay Daugherty, *Training Cyber Warriors: What Can Be Learned from Defense Language Training?*, Santa Monica, Calif.: RAND Corporation, RR-476-OSD, 2015. As of February 23, 2021:
https://www.rand.org/pubs/research_reports/RR476.html

Libicki, Martin C., David Senty, and Julia Pollak, *Hackers Wanted: An Examination of the Cybersecurity Labor Market*, Santa Monica, Calif.: RAND Corporation, RR-430, 2014. As of February 23, 2021:
https://www.rand.org/pubs/research_reports/RR430.html

Lim, Nelson, Abigail Haddad, Dwayne M. Butler, and Katheryn Giglio, *First Steps Toward Improving DoD STEM Workforce Diversity: Response to the 2012 Department of Defense STEM Diversity Summit*, Santa Monica, Calif.: RAND Corporation, RR-329-OSD, 2013. As of February 23, 2021:
https://www.rand.org/pubs/research_reports/RR329.html

Lim, Nelson, Abigail Haddad, and Lindsay Daugherty, *Implementation of the DoD Diversity and Inclusion Strategic Plan: A Framework for Change Through Accountability*, Santa Monica, Calif.: RAND Corporation, RR-333-OSD, 2013. As of February 23, 2021:
https://www.rand.org/pubs/research_reports/RR333.html

Lytell, Maria C., Kirsten M. Keller, Beth Katz, Jefferson P. Marquis, and Jerry M. Sollinger, *Diversity Leadership in the U.S. Department of Defense: Analysis of the Key Roles, Responsibilities, and Attributes of Diversity Leaders*, Santa Monica, Calif.: RAND Corporation, RR-1148-OSD, 2016. As of February 23, 2021:
https://www.rand.org/pubs/research_reports/RR1148.html

Lytell, Maria C., Susan G. Straus, Chad C. Serena, Geoffrey E. Grimm, James L. Doty III, Jennie W. Wenger, Andrea M. Abler, Andrew M. Naber, Clifford A. Grammich, and Eric S. Fowler, *Assessing Competencies and Proficiency of Army Intelligence Analysts Across the Career Life Cycle*, Santa Monica, Calif.: RAND Corporation, RR-1851-A, 2017. As of February 23, 2021:
https://www.rand.org/pubs/research_reports/RR1851.html

Markel, M. Wade, Jefferson P. Marquis, Peter Schirmer, Sean Robson, Lisa Saum-Manning, Katherine C. Hastings, Katharina Ley Best, Christina Panis, Alyssa Ramos, and Barbara Bicksler, *Career Development for the Department of Defense Security Cooperation Workforce*, Santa Monica, Calif.: RAND Corporation, RR-1846-OSD, 2018. As of February 23, 2021:
https://www.rand.org/pubs/research_reports/RR1846.html

Matthews, Miriam, Bruce R. Orvis, David Schulker, Kimberly Curry Hall, Abigail Haddad, Stefan Zavislan, and Nelson Lim, *Hispanic Representation in the Department of Defense Civilian Workforce: Trend and Barrier Analysis*, Santa Monica, Calif.: RAND Corporation, RR-1699-OSD, 2017. As of February 23, 2021:
https://www.rand.org/pubs/research_reports/RR1699.html

Matthews, Miriam, David Schulker, Kimberly Curry Hall, Abigail Haddad, and Nelson Lim, *Representation of Persons with Targeted Disabilities: An Analysis of Barriers to Employment in the Department of Defense Civilian Workforce*, Santa Monica, Calif.: RAND Corporation, RR-2297-OSD, 2018. As of February 23, 2021:
https://www.rand.org/pubs/research_reports/RR2297.html

Nataraj, Shanthi, Christopher Guo, Philip Hall-Partyka, Susan M. Gates, and Douglas Yeung, *Options for Department of Defense Total Workforce Supply and Demand Analysis: Potential Approaches and Available Data Sources*, Santa Monica, Calif.: RAND Corporation, RR-543-OSD, 2014. As of February 23, 2021:
https://www.rand.org/pubs/research_reports/RR543.html

National Security Agency Central Security Service, "National Centers of Academic Excellence in Cybersecurity," webpage, undated. As of July 24, 2020:
https://www.nsa.gov/resources/students-educators/centers-academic-excellence/

Paul, Christopher, Isaac R. Porche III, and Elliot Axelband, *The Other Quiet Professionals: Lessons for Future Cyber Forces from the Evolution of Special Forces*, Santa Monica, Calif.: RAND Corporation, RR-780-A, 2014. As of February 23, 2021:
https://www.rand.org/pubs/research_reports/RR780.html

Porche, Isaac R., III, Caolionn O'Connell, John S. Davis II, Bradley Wilson, Chad C. Serena, Tracy C. McCausland, Erin-Elizabeth Johnson, Brian D. Wisniewski, and Michael Vasseur, *Cyber Power Potential of the Army's Reserve Component*, Santa Monica, Calif.: RAND Corporation, RR-1490-A, 2017. As of February 23, 2021:
https://www.rand.org/pubs/research_reports/RR1490.html

Robson, Sean, Bonnie L. Triezenberg, Samantha E. DiNicola, Lindsey Polley, John S. Davis II, Maria C. Lytell, *Software Acquisition Workforce Initiative for the Department of Defense: Initial Competency Development and Preparation for Validation*, Santa Monica, Calif.: RAND Corporation, RR-3145-OSD, 2020. As of February 23, 2021:
https://www.rand.org/pubs/research_reports/RR3145.html

Ross, Shirley M., Rebecca Herman, Irina A. Chindea, Samantha E. Dinicola, and Amy Grace Donohue, *Optimizing the Contributions of Air Force Civilian STEM Workforce*, Santa Monica, Calif.: RAND Corporation, RR-4234-AF, 2020. As of February 23, 2021:
https://www.rand.org/pubs/research_reports/RR4234.html

Schmidt, Lara, Caolionn O'Connell, Hirokazu Miyake, Akhil R. Shah, Joshua William Baron, Geof Nieboer, Rose Jourdan, David Senty, Zev Winkelman, Louise Taggart, Susanne Sondergaard, and Neil Robinson, *Cyber Practices: What Can the U.S. Air Force Learn from the Commercial Sector?*, Santa Monica, Calif.: RAND Corporation, RR-847-AF, 2015. As of February 23, 2021:
https://www.rand.org/pubs/research_reports/RR847.html

Schulker, David, and Miriam Matthews, *Women's Representation in the U.S. Department of Defense Workforce: Addressing the Influence of Veterans' Employment*, Santa Monica, Calif.: RAND Corporation, RR-2458-OSD, 2018. As of February 23, 2021:
https://www.rand.org/pubs/research_reports/RR2458.html

Straus, Susan G., Tracy C. Krueger, Geoffrey E. Grimm, and Katheryn Giglio, *Malleability and Measurement of Army Leader Attributes: Personnel Development in the U.S. Army*, Santa Monica, Calif.: RAND Corporation, RR-1583-A, 2018. As of February 23, 2021:
https://www.rand.org/pubs/research_reports/RR1583.html

Straus, Susan G., Michael G. Shanley, Carra S. Sims, Bryan W. Hallmark, Anna Rosefsky Saavedra, Stoney Trent, and Sean Duggan, *Innovative Leader Development: Evaluation of the U.S. Army Asymmetric Warfare Adaptive Leader Program*, Santa Monica, Calif.: RAND Corporation, RR-504-A, 2014. As of February 23, 2021:
https://www.rand.org/pubs/research_reports/RR504.html

U.S. Department of Defense, *Summary of the 2018 National Defense Strategy: Sharpening the American Military's Competitive Edge*, Washington, D.C., 2018. As of January 10, 2020:
https://dod.defense.gov/Portals/1/Documents/pubs/2018-National-Defense-Strategy-Summary.pdf

U.S. Office of Personnel Management, "Human Capital Framework: Overview, Talent Management," webpage, undated. As of January 10, 2020:
https://www.opm.gov/policy-data-oversight/human-capital-framework/talent-management/#url=Overview

Wenger, Jennie W., Caolionn O'Connell, and Maria C. Lytell, *Retaining the Army's Cyber Expertise*, Santa Monica, Calif.: RAND Corporation, RR-1978-A, 2017. As of February 23, 2021:
https://www.rand.org/pubs/research_reports/RR1978.html

Werber, Laura, John A. Ausink, Lindsay Daugherty, Brian Phillips, Felix Knutson, and Ryan Haberman, *An Assessment of Gaps in Business Acumen and Knowledge of Industry Within the Defense Acquisition Workforce: A Report Prepared for the U.S. Department of Defense in Compliance with Section 843(c) of the Fiscal Year 2018 National Defense Authorization Act*, Santa Monica, Calif.: RAND Corporation, RR-2825-OSD, 2019. As of February 23, 2021:
https://www.rand.org/pubs/research_reports/RR2825.html

Werber, Laura, Paul W. Mayberry, Mark Doboga, and Diana Gehlhaus Carew, *Support for DoD Supervisors in Addressing Poor Employee Performance: A Holistic Approach*, Santa Monica, Calif.: RAND Corporation, RR-2665-OSD, 2018. As of February 23, 2021:
https://www.rand.org/pubs/research_reports/RR2665.html

The White House, *President's Management Agenda*, Washington, D.C., 2018. As of April 20, 2021:
https://trumpadministration.archives.performance.gov/PMA/Presidents_Management_Agenda.pdf